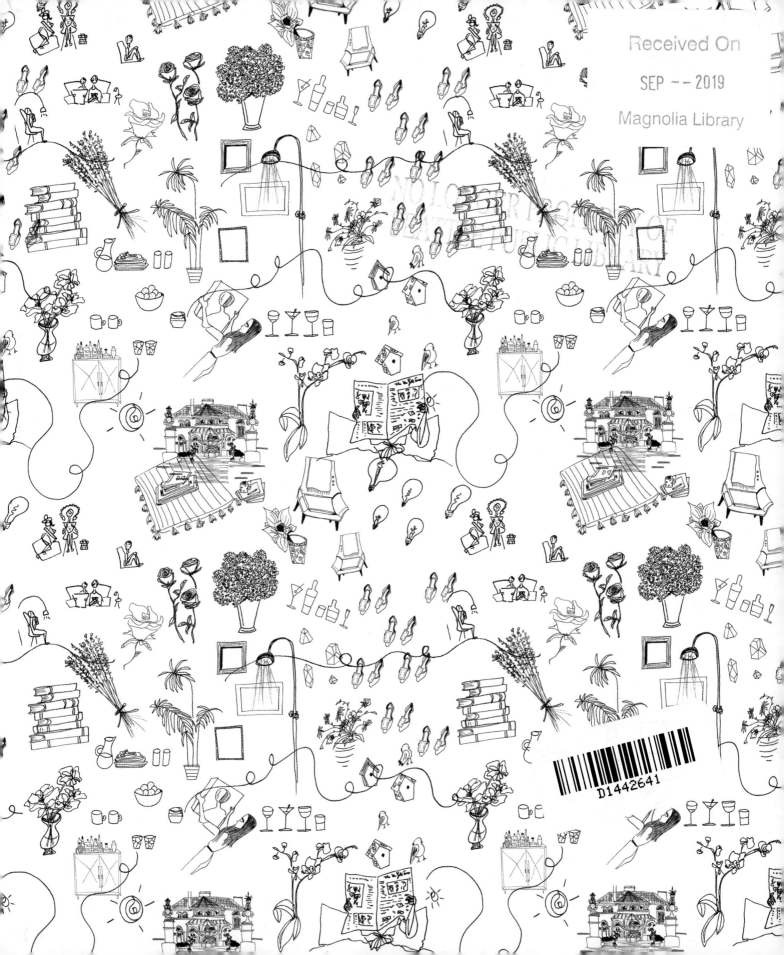

IN COMFORT AND STYLE

estee stanley

IN COMFORT AND STYLE

WRITTEN WITH CHRISTINA SHANAHAN

ILLUSTRATIONS BY CARLY KUHN

to bryan, teddy, and flora

Thank you for your love and support on this wild journey.
It's a crazy lifestyle that this job often requires,
and I couldn't do it without you.

to ashley

I've been so lucky to have the friendship and support
of a strong woman like you. You got me—and my home—through some
of the most challenging moments and I'm forever grateful.

contents

Ashley and I got to know each other at a magazine photo shoot, but she quickly became a close friend, one of my first home design clients, and my ultimate ride-or-die.

foreword

I first met Estee in 2002 during a fitting with my sister Mary-Kate for a *Rolling Stone* shoot. She had pulled the widest array of vintage, couture, high-end, and low-end garments. It immediately became obvious that we would be working with her as a stylist for many years to come because we were attracted to such similar things. But what captured me the most during this first of many fittings wasn't Estee's work as a fashion stylist but her impeccable style of home design. My sister and I had many impressive, creative, stylish women in our lives, but no one came close to Estee and her idiosyncratic self.

A few years later, when the time came to choose a decorator to work with on our first home, the one person who came to mind was Estee. The one problem was, she had never formally been hired to decorate a house. We didn't care, and we ultimately decided to take the risk. We wanted that magical thing you can't really put your finger on because it's not obvious or overt. We were going for a tone . . . a vibe . . . a feeling.

Over time, I came to realize that it is Estee's attention to detail that makes her homes special. Not the obvious details like trim or hardware but the ones that turn a space into an experience. It's the red etched crystal glasses she serves her drinks in, her lilac 1970s Murano chandelier that sparkles like a disco ball when the light hits it, and the Moroccan embroidered hand towels hanging in her bathroom. We wanted a vibe-y room in our own home that felt intimate yet glamorous, where guests could hang and let loose, much like the smoking room Estee has in her own house.

Estee creates alluring environments. We wanted her to show us both how to live and how to entertain in a space that felt like it was designed with an old-world approach, where quality of life and function come first. It is a very rare quality to come across. This is Estee's specialty, and I believe it's her love for entertaining in a great environment that drives her approach to design. Approachable, fun, humorous, creative, tasteful, and unpretentious are some of the characteristics that make me love her so much on both a personal and a professional level. Those qualities are what make her homes distinct and interesting.

Estee is one of a kind, and perhaps one of the craziest people I know. I'm grateful to have had the privilege of learning from her. She taught me that it's best to be uncompromising and take risks, because life is short. We might as well have fun while we can.

—ASHLEY OLSEN

introduction

When I moved out on my own, I went through a fairly typical progression of living arrangements: a shared rental apartment, which was so messy it mortified my mother every time she came over, then a condo—my first adult home purchase—where I slept on a mattress on the floor with a billiards table for a dining surface. But as a person who craves both creativity and constant change, I was never one for small-space living. I was in love with the European-style architecture in LA's Hancock Park neighborhood, yet the multimillion-dollar abodes typically found in this area were way beyond my budget.

Eventually, I happened upon a 4,500-square-foot duplex on the edge of Hancock Park, and I took a leap of faith. It was a two-family home at the time, so I had a tenant living downstairs while I occupied the second-floor apartment, which featured green popcorn walls and giant, unsightly windows. To make matters worse, I went through a devastating breakup with my then boyfriend, now husband, two weeks after I moved in. It was hard to tell which was a bigger mess—my personal life or the massive fixer-upper I now had on my hands.

I always say that the evolution of a home renovation inevitably mirrors the homeowner's current mental state, and mine was no exception. My house became a metaphor for getting my life together and figuring out what I really wanted to do. It took me a year and half to save enough money to lose the tenant and make the house a single-family home. My close friend and styling client at the time, Ashley Olsen, moved in with me, and we started renovating room by room. We stayed in the house during construction and spent our days staining doors and moving couches up and down stairs—all by ourselves. I added a staircase and reconfigured the living room. At night, we mixed cocktails and talked about what I would ultimately do with my dream home.

After eight months of work, I emerged with a house I loved, an incomparable friendship with Ashley, and a restored relationship with the man I would marry, with whom I knew I wanted to share the space and raise a family. What I learned is that sometimes you have to demolish every wall to rebuild in the way you truly want to live. My husband and I still live in the same Hancock Park home, and, ten years later, we've made very few changes to the house's

My earliest memory of a home is that of my grandparents' house. Today, many of my grandmother's pieces are permanent fixtures in my family's home, and I strive to create spaces that blend the old with the new, the sentimental with the chic.

structure. I'll revamp paint colors and décor, but the bones remain. Now, as a designer, I never want my clients to invest in something they won't still love in ten years—or more—and that principle guides every project I take on.

Clients come to me with a huge compilation of ideas, and I have to put the ingredients together to make their visions work in a real-life way. When I design, I look at both the aesthetic of the client and the soul of the house, then decide how to blend those two energies. It's a magical combination. I wrote this book with the goal of unpacking my design philosophy and breaking down the styling tricks that have become the signature of some of my all-time favorite homes. Whether you're looking to transform your own abode or just make a few simple tweaks, I hope it inspires you to create a space that evokes comfort, style, and ease. Once that casual elegance is achieved, I know that I've done my job.

living

When I was growing up, it was the era of the "formal" living room, where you couldn't so much as have a drink without fearing for your life. Couches were simply for sitting completely still, which was a major challenge when your skin was becoming one with the thick layer of protective plastic. Chic, right? Most adults I knew when I was young lived in a shroud of sofa covers and throw pillows that you weren't allowed to lean on—except for my grandma Florence. My family and I spent a lot of time at my grandparents' one-story home, and I have the best memories of actually *relaxing* in the living room. She had extremely polished, retro taste. (The *Mad Men*–era vibes extended well into the 1980s in that house.) The formal brass-and-white décor featured a baby grand piano and a huge white couch that we basically lived on. Despite the light color, she didn't worry about us damaging the couch. She wanted people to be at ease and let their guard down while they were in her home. I inherited that couch; it now sits in my own living room—albeit reupholstered—and trust me: fewer accidents happen when you're relaxed and not stressed about messing something up. I can't remember a Friday night when my grandmother didn't have at least thirty people over for Shabbat dinner, and it's from her that I inherited my drive to create homes that are made for entertaining and letting loose. Every room should have a purpose, and since the living room is typically one of the first spaces you see when you walk into a home, it's the best indicator of how someone lives.

The two items that anchor the living room in my Hancock Park
home are the large white sofa and the baby grand piano, both of
which belonged to my grandmother. Despite the sofa's light
color, my family and I sit on the couch all the time—a tribute to
exactly how she wanted us to live: in comfort and style.

feel free to splurge

More guests will obviously see your living room than your bedrooms, den, and—in most cases—even your kitchen, so you're justified in using a good portion of your budget to make it exactly what you want. Invest in furniture that you'll have for years and a couch that feels comfortable enough to lie on for hours. In a living room, the couch is the showcase piece. It's the center of attention, and often the element that sets the tone for the rest of the room, so let this be your priority.

If the room feels boxy or boring, bump it up a bit by installing crown or rail molding. (Consider raw wood molding for a more rustic look.) Paint the walls in slightly contrasting shades of the same color to add dimension. If you have casement or double-hung windows, add drapes to provide texture and make them feel finished. If you have more elaborate custom stationary windows or floor-to-ceiling picture windows, skip the drapes and focus on beautifully accessorizing the surrounding area inside the room and the view that they overlook.

A great way to add dimension to a small or boxy living room—like the one in this Malibu home I designed in collaboration with Brigette Romanek—is to think about how you're framing the doors, windows, and entryway. Don't be afraid to go for something nontraditional, like dark moldings or casings, to draw attention.

OPPOSITE: The living room is an ideal space for showcasing special big-ticket items, such as a custom sofa or a set of vintage armchairs. ABOVE: I typically avoid incorporating televisions and electronics into formal living rooms, but if it's a space where the homeowner wants to relax and binge-watch their favorite shows, then a sleek built-in unit above a fireplace or on an accent wall is a way of incorporating a screen so that it doesn't detract from the space.

Create a cozy reading nook by adding a chair and an end table to a low-traffic area to ensure that every corner of the space gets utilized. Accessorizing each nook allows you to design vignettes for special pieces you've invested in that don't necessarily have a place in the central area of the room.

All the pieces don't have to match in order to work well together. Aim for a diverse mix of items that fall within the same palette to create a look that is tied together yet unique.

think sustainable

The reason I love shopping for vintage furniture and accessories isn't just because of the one-of-a-kind pieces I come across—it's also a great way to reduce your carbon footprint by giving something another life in your home. Similarly, I never throw away a piece of furniture if there's a chance it can be repurposed. Maybe that bench no longer suits your entryway, but it could be stained to look entirely new and become the perfect living room coffee table. When accessorizing, try to stay away from anything made with plastic due to the environmental impact, and if you're doing construction, ask your contractor to work with reclaimed materials.

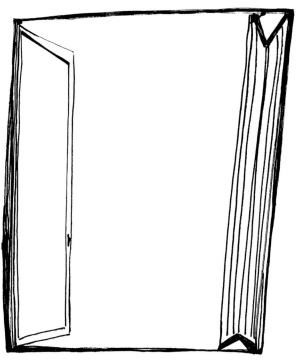

One of my favorite ways to reduce the carbon footprint in a home is to reupholster chairs or other pieces of furniture rather than simply throw away the old and bring in the new. A fresh texture, print, or color on an existing piece can change the entire vibe of the room.

Objects like books and small
sculptures—or even ottomans and
end tables—are easy to replace
in order to give any living room a quick
update or a fresh look without
doing a major overhaul. You can also
move them from room to room.

make it easy to remix

I'm obsessed with entertaining (more on that later), and my idea of a perfect weekend includes fifteen friends relaxing on my front patio. I love designing spaces where you don't have to do major preparation to get your house "ready" for guests. Accent chairs are always a worthy investment; you can get unique, inexpensive ones and easily move them from room to room. Line them up against the wall in your dining room for an eclectic look when they aren't being used, and push them into the living room if you have guests so that everyone feels like they have a place to sit.

Pillows and throws add comfort to the space. If your couches are packed with accent pillows, toss a few large ones on the floor propped against the couch to make space—this way no one worries about messing up your "arrangement" if they want to sit down. As a bonus, anyone who wants to stretch out after dinner can sit on the floor with a comfy pillow against their back.

When it comes to accent pillows, more is more—and not only because they're so crucial to refreshing the look and feel of a space. They also allow guests to feel comfortable while you entertain. When I'm at home in the Hamptons, I also love seasonal floral arrangements for making every room look fresh.

train your wild things

Living freely and comfortably in your living room doesn't mean destroying your living room. You work hard to achieve a certain aesthetic, so you should want the results to last. The home is a haven, and you have to teach your pets and your children to respect it. Train your dog or cat not to jump up on the couch if you have a gorgeous light or delicate fabric that you care about protecting. Cats are my nightmare because they'll scale any surface, but I always recommend setting up their supplies in an area like the basement or a mudroom so they have an indoor home base that isn't on top of your antique bookshelf.

I don't believe in designating the living room as off-limits for kids; I would rather set boundaries and make rules. My kids know they can't come into our living room with crayons, paint, or chocolate ice cream—only water. Instead of allowing free rein, dedicate a noncentral space in your house as a free area where children can play, be messy, and not worry about getting in trouble for it. My kids have a playroom where there are no rules. It's home to my daughter's hideous play teepee (her uncle bought it simply to torture me), which is basically coated in glitter and makeup.

When parents say that they "can't" have certain pieces in their home because their children may ruin them, it makes me crazy. Whether it's a delicate glass coffee table or a light-colored couch, you have to set the standard for your kids' behavior rather than forgo having pieces that capture your personal style.

dim the lights

I always opt for dimmers because lower lighting makes everyone feel young and beautiful—and when you're feeling good, you're ready to relax. (I know it sounds shallow, but it's no joke!) No one wants to walk into a house that's lit up like Times Square. I also believe that the living room should have light fixtures, not just overhead recessed cans. You can find a fixture to fit any taste, and it's an opportunity to inject major personality into a space. A statement fixture can be an indicator of what kind of mood to expect from the entire home.

If natural light flows freely into your living room, casting a nice glow at every hour of the day, then how lucky are you? But if not, position light fixtures that are designed as mini works of art in areas you want to showcase, like over a bar or near a gallery wall of favorite paintings.

Lighting fixtures are among my all-time favorite accessories to shop for because they add so much personality to a space. If you have a large room with a high ceiling, more is more. Choose different shapes, sizes, and colors with similar hardware to keep the grouping looking dynamic yet cohesive.

When choosing furniture, consider the scale of the items around your central pieces, like couches and coffee tables. If the room is large, choose proportionally large lamps, end tables, and artwork.

extend the cool vibes

I may be one of the few people in the world who has friends who still smoke, but one of my favorite rooms in my entire home is the smoking room. It's a tiny area right at the front of the house with French doors that transform it into an indoor/outdoor space when opened. I lined the walls with bookcases and worn-in leather furniture to make the room feel moody and dark. My husband and I hang out in there when we want to feel like adults, and it's always packed when we have parties. (The secret? We keep booze on the bookshelves.)

I've done a few of these smoking rooms for clients, and it's a perfect example of why you should aim to give every space beyond the living room a clear purpose and its own inviting vibe. Some clients have requested bar rooms for a space where they can play cards and puff on cigars; some, solariums, so that they can relax in a comfy chair surrounded by greenery; and some, dining rooms with tables surrounded by armchairs and banquettes for the comfiest meal hangouts ever. Do whatever it takes to ensure that you'll find pleasure in every square foot of your home.

OPPOSITE: Think about what you love to do in your home. My husband and I constantly have friends over to enjoy good drinks and good conversation, so we created a smoking room that's strictly an adult hangout. I've been asked to create many similar spaces for clients over the years. PAGES 40–41: Layering multiple shades of one color or color family is a cool way to make a statement without going too wild.

I've had clients ask me to create some pretty wild fantasy spaces—everything from game rooms to grottos—to extend their living areas. The floor-to-ceiling windows and glass patio doors of this Malibu home I designed with Brigette Romanek are perfect for bringing the fun of the outdoors inside, where it can be enjoyed year-round.

inspiration

When it comes to creating cozy, comfortable spaces, like this one in Lea Michele's home, many of my mood boards start with natural materials like raw woods and textured linen. I add fabric swatches for the tactile elements that will ultimately contribute warmth to the space, like rugs, throws, and pillows.

shades of white   shades of   pop of
                     gray   green

46

palette

n invitation into someone's home is an invitation to relax. When I have friends over, I want to give them a chance to leave behind their daily hustle, forget the outside world, and focus on the pure bliss that comes from good conversation and—inevitably—good wine. Moving from room to room should feel like the continuation of a soothing narrative, both for visitors and for you. The most impactful way to master this transition is through color. You have to be a real expert in color to do a house where every room is painted a different hue. Although I've been experimenting more with color recently, it's not my true forte, so I tend to create a more cohesive look with neutrals.

I always prefer a palette of many shades of white—and, yes, if you've ever been to a paint store, you know that white does in fact come in multiple shades. White is a dreamy color, and its purposefully calming tones immediately transport you to a more serene mindset. White makes everything feel crisp and clean. When you have a white canvas for your home, you give yourself more freedom to experiment with color in how you accessorize.

Light neutrals that evoke serenity are key in bedrooms. At the end of the day, you want a space that helps you drift off to sleep— not a bold statement that makes you feel energized.

A neutral palette doesn't necessarily mean light shades. Deep earth tones, like espresso and cognac, can add cozy warmth to a room—these shades work especially well for dens and dining spaces.

accent white walls

The brightest shades of white should be
reserved for kitchens, dining rooms,
and bathrooms. Those are the spaces that
you want to appear extra spacious (an
effect that wall-to-wall white can help
achieve) and to give off squeaky-clean vibes.
I once had a client who insisted on doing
red and royal blue, and it felt chaotic to me.
There are significantly more subtle ways
that you can achieve a wow-inducing effect.
My own kitchen is all white, including the
cabinets and marble, so to add some interest,
I found a blue-and-white table to offset
the neutrals and immediately draw attention.

When it comes to bedrooms, creamy
off-whites will make you feel like you're
sleeping in a cloud. For living rooms,
I often go for shades that are between off-
white and very light gray. I recently
used a pale dusty rose paint in a living
room, and I loved how it turned out. Color
on a large scale makes most homeowners
nervous, and freshening up your living
room shouldn't make you want to reach for
the Xanax; so keep the color manageable.

*An easy way to break up white space
on a wall is to create a simple, ever-evolving
photo collage. Above the banquette in my
kitchen, I assembled a grid where we pin family
snaps, postcards, and sketches we love.*

Color can be used to give the illusion of more space, which is particularly helpful in kitchens, where you want everything to feel bright, airy, and spotless. Choose white or light wood cabinets, complemented by bright overhead light fixtures, to open up the room.

There's something incredibly relaxing about layering different shades of white. Pairing light-colored furniture with draperies and accent tables that are just a few shades darker and in different textures creates a rich yet soothing look.

mary-kate olsen interviews ellen pompeo

MARY-KATE OLSEN What's one thing you own that you're obsessed with, but Estee can't stand?

ELLEN POMPEO Throw pillows! We fight over pillows because we have totally different taste in accessories. We have literal pillow fights.

MARY-KATE OLSEN What's the Estee advice you always swear by?

ELLEN POMPEO I always take her advice when we come across something really special while shopping. She'll say, "This is amazing and you have to have it." I always listen, and I'm always happy I did.

MARY-KATE OLSEN The Estee advice you didn't take but wish you had?

ELLEN POMPEO I can't put that in print!

MARY-KATE OLSEN Do you have a favorite Estee moment?

ELLEN POMPEO Once I was in a shop and I picked up a beautiful gold tray and said, "I have to have this." The shop owner told me that Estee had already purchased one for me, but strangely enough, the tray never appeared. Until one night when I slept in Estee's guest room. I looked at the bedside table and . . . boom! There it was. I went to sleep that night with a smile on my face. Oh, Estee.

color and light

Regardless of how much color—or how little—you want to infuse into your own life, there is one often-overlooked point that I'm constantly whispering to clients as they painstakingly choose paint and accessories: do not neglect the lighting. Lighting must not be an afterthought, because it can completely change how color looks. Bright overhead lighting can have a very harsh impact on paint and fabrics. Relaxing white paints have the opposite effect, and no one needs surgical lighting when they're cozied up in loungewear, ready to unwind. Bright overheads can also change the tones in furniture, making your entire palette look out of sync. Put your overhead lighting on dimmers and supplement it with chandeliers, decorative lamps, and sconces— you can't go wrong with a subtle, sexy glow.

PREVIOUS: If you have windows or patio doors that overlook a scenic area or open onto greenery, make it a part of your décor by keeping the walls unadorned and choosing simple drapes that unveil the natural beauty, as Ellen Pompeo and I did in her living room. RIGHT: A palette of relaxing whites necessitates overhead lighting that is soft and enhances the tones of your walls, furniture, and textiles rather than detracting from the look with a harsh shine. Skip recessed cans in favor of a combination of table lamps, sconces, and beautiful overhead fixtures.

My favorite color choice for a bedroom is creamy off-white.
Consider this when picking paint, fabrics for your furnishings, and
bed linens. Sasha Alexander's home renovation was a complete
transformation from the original design, so my goal was to ensure that
each room felt like the ultimate in relaxation.

when to challenge color standards

There are times when taking a risk with color can have a major payoff. Here's how to do it without risking remorse.

IGNORE YOUR PAINT SWATCH IMPULSES

When it comes to painting in color, a bold move can seem like a great idea if you're looking at a two-inch square or a tiny photo online. It's hard to understand the scale of how something will look in real life when your point of reference is itty-bitty. Many clients come to me with dreams of an orange accent wall, but they don't understand that tangerine doesn't quite translate in life size. The worst-case scenario? They insist on it, it looks crazy, and they beg me for an explanation of why "we" did this. Commit to buying enough of the color to see it in the space at various times of day (not just a swatch—you should paint at least a 24" by 12" area to get the full impact), or play it safe and don't choose a bold statement color.

GO GREEN

I stay away from bold colors as much as possible—except for green, which can be incredibly cool as an accent color. I had the same simple white fireplace in my Los Angeles house for years, and during a recent renovation, I decided to replace it with something funky: green abalone tile. It took my husband and me about a month of staring at the thing and questioning whether we'd lost our minds before we got used to it, but whenever guests come in and go bananas over the result, I know it was worthwhile to add this pop of primary color.

LET SMALL SPACES BE RULE-FREE

If you have bold color dreams and you want a space where you can indulge them, do it in your bathroom, office, or walk-in closet. These are small rooms, and no one is congregating in there, so you may as well experiment. Paint them a funky color, do an accent wall, do as much as you possibly can with accessories. I love when I walk into a small bathroom and it looks like a jewel box, with a blend of different materials on the walls, floor, and surfaces, as opposed to a bathroom where only the shower is marble and everything else is very neutral.

PREVIOUS: Though recently I've been playing with bold color, I'm much more comfortable with neutrals. This update to my own living room was a major departure from my comfort zone, but I love how the green tile fireplace subtly brings out the jewel tones in the room's accessories. LEFT: In the Hamptons, I'm always so inspired by the vibrant use of color inside and outside the area's beachfront houses that I've incorporated many of the hues into my own Sagaponack home. Rather than use wallpaper, I painted stripes onto these bedroom walls in a natural hue that reminds me of the beach.

a pop of color

Since I tend to obsess over white and off-white canvases for my homes, I usually begin incorporating color into the foreground of the space. When I meet with new clients, I find out what colors they gravitate toward by looking at their Pinterest boards, the art that they own, and even how they dress. Based on their personal favorites, I choose the "theme" colors that I'll subtly incorporate throughout the house. Say, for example, the homeowners vibe with greens and blues—I'll source a rug in which these tones are prominent, and perhaps do green tile for the kitchen countertops. To complement these hues and create a unique look, oak moldings can add further dimension due to the dark shade of this untreated wood. I find that faded tones work best for larger pieces, like rugs and drapes. Sometimes, a cool printed chair in a muted pattern is the perfect thing to give a room some substance. The best place to play with bolder colors is in your small accessories. Pillows and throws are quick, easy, and fairly inexpensive to change out or supplement.

I've been using neutrals and muted hues for so long that now I'm starting to experiment. It's fun to be a little more adventurous when I'm designing vacation homes or working on my own Hamptons house. One of my favorite things to see when driving through the Hamptons is that even though all the houses are white with vibrant painted shutters, all the doors are different bright colors—it's like cruising through a watercolor painting. Beach towns and tropical locales just lend themselves to color play. I added a floral print couch to my Hamptons house—the background is white and the pattern is predominantly faded emerald green and purple. The white still acts as an anchor, and the couch is placed on top of a faded black rug.

Layering shades of pale pink can infuse life into a room through color without making it feel chaotic or overly bright. The monochrome look begs to be punctuated by a few brightly colored accessories for a truly whimsical vibe.

Pops of color often work incredibly well in small doses. If a homeowner favors vibrant pinks or zesty oranges, I may steer them to go all out in a home office, like this one I designed with Mat Sanders (above), or in a smaller space rather than a large common area.

the color
rule to live by

THINK CAREFULLY ABOUT THAT BRIGHTLY COLORED COUCH

Trust me, it will limit you. All your options for accessorizing become much, much more narrow. If you sink your budget into a cherry-red sectional, be sure to surround it with more neutral, muted pieces that will give you flexibility in remixing the accent items.

Bright pops of primary color were integrated into the home of Pressed Juicery founder Hedi Gores though artwork, textiles, and interchangeable pillows and throws.

I obsess over emerald, and these Brenda Antin chaise longues in Jillian and Patrick Dempsey's home complement the natural greenery both inside and outside the house. We opted for muted tones for the rest of the furnishings in the room to let these verdant beauties stand out.

inspiration

When it comes to doing bold color accents, I often gravitate toward green as a primary
hue. It's rich and bright yet still a shade found in nature, so it mixes perfectly with neutrals
and understated prints.

styling

there's no doubt that seeing someone naked is a very personal experience, but I can assure you that spending months working in someone's home is a much deeper study in intimacy. When I was a stylist, a regular part of my day was helping people get dressed, which required me to get up close and personal with my clients to understand their figure and what flattered every inch of their frame. But when you're in someone's house for a renovation, you see every detail of their lives play out in front of you like a film. You see the true dynamics of the relationships within a family, and who people are at their core—you bear witness to the very best and the very worst. I've even played the role of marriage counselor during construction. From the first meeting with design clients through the end of the project, many facets of the homeowners' personalities come to light.

I always say that every home has a personality, and I get so much inspiration from the personalities of the people I surround myself with, from close friends to clients past and present.

Just as jewelry and handbags punctuate an outfit,
accessories are the finishing touches that add flair to a room.
From pillows to wall sconces to decorative objects placed
on tables or shelves, these details are just as important as the
layout of a room or big-ticket furniture purchases.

home style

Because of how much clients are forced to let me in during a renovation, I've leaned on my styling background to help me navigate the design process. My goal is to make the people I'm working with feel as comfortable as possible so that we can get the best result: a killer home. Sourcing rugs, fabrics, and other textiles and accessories to complement a space isn't all that different from styling a fully accessorized outfit, but the stakes are significantly higher. It's more permanent and way more expensive. If you don't like a pair of pants I put you in, no problem. Take them off, and I'll find you another cute option. If you hate the infinity pool I've just built into your backyard, then we have a bigger—and more costly—issue.

Designing a home is just as much a study in psychology as it is in aesthetics. It's so important to keep your personality and personal style in mind when you're making your selections. I've designed the homes of many clients and friends I used to style, including Ashley and Mary-Kate Olsen, Lea Michele, Jessica Biel, and Ellen Pompeo. Each one has a different comfort level, and I knew from the choices they made on the red carpet how far they would be willing to push the envelope in their home.

Jessica's wedding is a prime example of how my worlds merge. Having known her and her husband, Justin Timberlake, for years, I planned the event with them, and I also styled her bridal look. Her wedding dress was an incredible pink floral Giambattista Valli gown, and although the color was easy to see in photos, the floral pattern was much more prominent in person. It was so nontraditional that every time we did a fitting, we would all stand there in awe of how uniquely stunning it was. Jessica is a risk-taker, and the dress worked out incredibly well. Following those fittings, I went and found gorgeous floral fabrics and used them to reupholster a couch. If I hadn't found that dress for her, I would never have designed that sofa.

Peering into a client's closet for the prints and colors they favor—as we did for Lea Michele's entryway—is an indicator of what type of home accents they will prefer. Classic stripes tend to translate in both spaces.

PREVIOUS: Chairs are the shoes of the home. You can take some liberties and easily move them from room to room to remix your décor. I'll often upholster a chair in a bold print to turn it into a statement piece, much as I would add a funky shoe to a classic dress to make an outfit shine. ABOVE AND RIGHT: Jessica Biel's wedding gown featured a very intricate floral print. We took a risk with it, but it looked so special and glam that it ultimately inspired me to do a floral couch in a Hamptons home.

A killer bag from Gucci's Cruise 2017 collection (above) inspired me to think about how impactful the image of a serpent can be against a bold print. That same year, I sourced this Fornasetti table (opposite) for hairstylist Tracey Cunningham and her family.

a personal aesthetic

Just as someone's lifestyle affects what they wear, it's also very closely tied to how they want their home to look and feel. The way we dress is often an indicator of how we want to be perceived. Your personal aesthetic weaves its way into many areas of your life, and the home is no exception. If someone tends to wear minimalistic, gender-neutral clothing, their home décor is likely to be streamlined and curated. Those who are constantly stepping out in bold colors and patterns, on the other hand, are more likely to want a green velvet sofa and funky wallpaper. It's not a literal interpretation—just because you wear Dolce & Gabbana doesn't mean you'll want floor-to-ceiling printed curtains that mimic your favorite column gown. Rather, it is about the big picture of what excites you aesthetically and makes you feel inspired.

Lea Michele is the perfect example of a client whose style reflects her personality— she's very fashion savvy, and for her home, we opted for looks that were classic and sexy. When you walk into her living room, you immediately feel like you're entering her world. Her décor is elevated and sophisticated yet cozy and approachable. She's so on point with her aesthetic that I always joke she would be the greatest design assistant I could ever have. Sharp, mature, and on top of her game like no one else I know, Lea became my project manager when we worked on her homes. If a couch was meant to be delivered at 7:00 a.m., I would get a call at 6:59 asking where it was . . . even though I had already emailed three confirmations. (Love you, Lea!)

This 1970s-inspired look from Rachel Zoe's Spring 2018 collection (above) is pure green goodness. Clients who gravitate toward bold designer prints for their wardrobe are often willing to take a risk on a bold print statement in the home, as shown in the bathroom opposite.

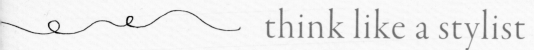

think like a stylist

When you peel back the layers of the design process, crafting the perfect space looks a lot like styling a gorgeous ensemble. The logistics are everything, and the method will influence the results. There are a few guiding principles that also apply to creating a space that you'll never want to leave.

AVOID THE DIRTY WORK

Stylists who work with celebrities ensure that their clients are never involved in the minutiae: calling in samples, having garments tailored, and all the fine details that come before a fitting. It's hard to understand what the final vision is if you're seeing only bits and pieces, and that can cause undue anxiety when there's still a ways to go to reach the results. The same applies to the construction phase of a renovation. I always advise homeowners to find another place to stay after we break ground. Aside from being unpleasant and inconvenient, living in a construction zone puts you in a mental state that is problematic. There might not be anywhere for you to go when you wake up. You might be forced to get ready in an unsightly, unsanitary bathroom. You're frustrated by seeing the contractors work and wondering why things aren't getting done faster. When you live in the midst of it, you can't help yourself from asking constant questions. Find somewhere else to stay, and check in on the renovation periodically—stop by at the end of each week and see how much has been done rather than come in daily and focus on what *hasn't* been completed.

FOCUS ON THE BIG PICTURE

Doing things piecemeal is the biggest waste of money. You will absolutely end up spending more and having superfluous materials if you try to pick up items here and there before finalizing the design. You're essentially flushing money right down the toilet that's waiting to be installed. If you go shopping for earring options before you know what dress you're wearing, you'll end up with five pairs that you don't need. In the same way, if you see a "deal" on tile before your bathroom design is complete, you'll be stuck with a pile of ceramic extras that you'll need to find a place to store—and they will not fit in your jewelry box. The best way to avoid this problem is to wait until you've fleshed out a plan for the full vision to start making decisions about the details.

TRUST YOUR TRIBE

It takes a village to pull together a red-carpet look. As a stylist, I worked with high-profile clients, so I was fortunate in that I was always able to secure the pieces I wanted; but it took a lot of energy and patience. Imagine thirty stylists calling a designer for one dress and then waiting around for the PR team to decide which person gets to wear it. I'm still confused about why they have only one sample line. Once you have the dress, there's the task of coordinating with the hairstylist and makeup artist to make sure each part of the look complements the others. When you're doing a home, there are more pieces to work with and the options are limitless, but it's similar in that you have to trust the other team members on all aspects and rely on the expertise of each individual. I'm not a plumber, and I'm not an electrician, but it's important for us to work as a team to get a project finished. If you're doing a DIY project or teaming up with a partner or significant other on a renovation, the best way to collaborate is for each of you to act as a lead on different elements of the process. If you're spearheading the construction, let your partner take the lead on furniture selection and décor.

RESPECT THE TIMELINE

Just like styling, designing a home happens in a very particular sequence. You're not going to start with a bracelet and build an entire outfit around it. Similarly, there's an order to how you renovate, remodel, and redesign, and it's more important to follow this order than to line up professionals based on their earliest availability. If expensive new marble countertops are installed before the electrical work and drywall repairs happen, you'll end up with three guys drilling and sanding all over the gorgeous counters. You may want to schedule work based on expediency, but it will ultimately extend the timeline of your project when you have to go back and fix damage or do patch repairs.

When a homeowner opts for clean, minimal outfits as a
signature of their personal aesthetic, it's often an
indicator that they will follow suit with their home decor.
Soothing white tile and walls and raw wood accents
can beautifully articulate that style.

Watabe Yukichi

DRIES VAN NOTEN

Interiors | Atelier AM

ICONS OF VINTAGE FASHION

mary-kate olsen
interviews lea michele

MARY-KATE OLSEN Estee wanted me to ask for your favorite room in the house to have sex in . . . so I'm going to ask you other questions instead.

LEA MICHELE I'm laughing out loud.

MARY-KATE OLSEN Why Estee Stanley?

LEA MICHELE Estee is one of the most iconic and fascinating people I've ever met. I had the pleasure of working with Estee for years as my stylist, and we put together some major fashion moments. I basically lived in her house and loved her style, so it was a no-brainer that Estee would design my first home. She created the most incredible, unique, and cozy design for my little West Hollywood cottage. When I moved into my second house, she had more room to play with and really transformed the space into something special. She's always encouraging my imagination and turning rooms into creative ideas that I would never have seen coming but absolutely love.

MARY-KATE OLSEN I love a good Estee story. Can you tell me a favorite moment you experienced during the design process?

LEA MICHELE They are too many stories from my years working with Estee. But I've given myself the title of her most challenging client because I push her limits by forcing her to style my homes within a set timeframe (her worst nightmare) and a set budget (the horror). I'm pretty sure I've given her more gray hairs than Tracey Cunningham can cover up. She must love me a lot because she always gets it done. She even stuck with me when I went through a phase of wanting everything pink, only to change my mind and opt for black and white with rock-and-roll posters everywhere instead.

MARY-KATE OLSEN How many people who worked for Estee have quit or been fired since you've known her?

LEA MICHELE Let's just say I've deleted a lot of "Estee Stanley Assistant" numbers from my phone over the years. And to answer your first question . . . the bathroom. Duh.

seasonal accents

Although my job no longer centers on couture gowns and runway shows, I always wonder how I can translate seasonal trends and major designer moments into the home space. If there's a crazy-cool moment that can make a statement, I'll find a way to work it into a design as an accent piece. When Isabel Marant became a household name several years ago, I did a lot of accessories in the homes I was designing that looked quite bohemian. The blankets had pom-poms or tassels, and it was a way of weaving in what was happening in the fashion world. I also love dramatic transformations. I'll take an amazing chair that has a classic shape (Brenda Antin's chairs are a favorite), then find a bold fabric inspired by a runway look to upholster it in. Upholstery is something that you can always change to give an accent piece an entirely different vibe.

Get inspired to accessorize your home as you would your favorite outfit. That dress you wear season after season—the one that makes you feel beautiful and confident each time you put it on—is your staple, but you can still remix it with jewelry and a new pair of pumps. Similarly, you'll love coming home to the living room or den that much more if you keep it fresh with seasonal favorites.

A few times a year, I evaluate in which small ways I can refresh each room in my home without drastically changing the inherent design details. For example, in the Hamptons, I look for arrangements featuring flowers that are native to the East Coast to infuse color and life into my living room. PAGES 102–103: In my closet, my eye travels to the classic pieces and big-ticket purchases that I wear year after year. I style them in fresh ways to reflect seasonal trends, and the same is true for my home staples . . . it's all about reinventing the mainstays.

life can be your mood board

The trick to creating a truly dynamic space is pulling inspiration from
every part of your life. The shapes and patterns you see in nature, a swatch of
fabric from an old dress that you haven't been able to part with, or even the
lining of an envelope you've torn off can be the springboard for a gorgeous
home. The more tactile your inspiration, the more accurately an interior designer
will be able to translate your aesthetic into tangible pieces. When I begin a
relationship with a new client, the process of decoding what inspires him or her
can take weeks. There's an exploratory phase during which we look through
favorite images of other spaces and break down the most appealing parts of each one.

I give everyone I work with one chance to show me their Pinterest boards.
Pinterest is a great tool for discovery, but ultimately everything that you'll find
on the platform is repurposed. I see the same images and the same designs over
and over, and as a designer, it's my job to play the DJ and remix ideas rather than
clone them. I never want a client to feel like he or she is living in a duplication . . .
it's much more satisfying to collaborate on a space that is uniquely personal.
Additionally, the result is not always harmonious when you are pulling inspiration
images from many different sources. A Victorian couch from one space and
an eclectic lamp from another may be incredible pieces individually but would
not necessarily make sense together in a room. The best approach is to gather
several images that all convey a similar style so that you can define your aesthetic,
then zero in on the individual elements that you love within each. This
approach allows for more flexibility when it comes time to translate the look
into your real life.

I typically start my first mood board for a client before I'm even hired for the
job. For this stage, I'll pull from projects that I've done in the past so that
if the homeowner gravitates toward any element, I can speak to exactly how it
was created and what I used. If you're working with a designer on your own
project, it's wise to go into a first meeting with examples you like from his or
her own work—you'll leave with a better understanding of what can be adapted
to your home.

Once I begin a job, my mood boards become more specific, and I create one for
each room. This time, however, I'm not solely populating the board with
pictures . . . now it's all about materials. As we explore these textures and surfaces
together, I start to learn to speak the client's language. Someone may say they
gravitate toward "warm" spaces and be referring to warm colors. Another could use
"warm" to refer to a cozy space, and yet another person could quite literally mean
that they want a fireplace. The most difficult part of translating your inspiration into
reality can be having the foresight—and patience—to wait for it to come together.

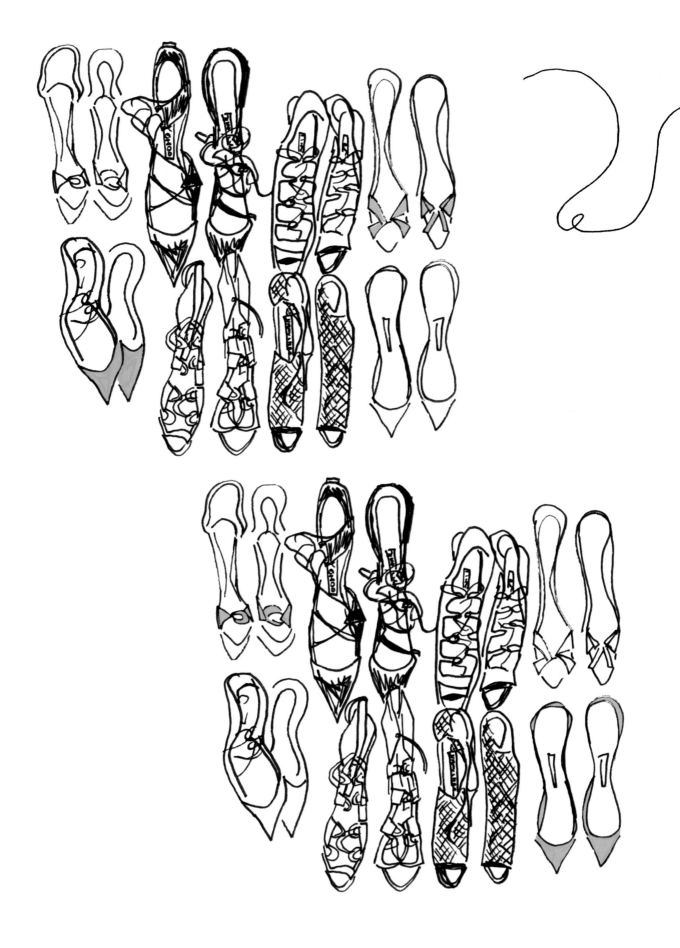

collecting

a s you infuse your personal style into your home, accessories will inevitably start to accumulate, and your affinity for certain objects will make itself clear—perhaps too clear. I don't consider myself a true hoarder, but I did grow up with one. My mom went through a phase where her collection of vintage perfume bottles was so vast that you couldn't find enough space to put a Q-tip down on her bathroom countertops. You could have filled a semitruck with these tiny treasures. The bottles overflowed into every nook and cranny of the room—it got to a point where she lined them up on the deck of her bathtub because she ran out of space elsewhere. If you're stepping over collectibles just to find a clear path to the shower, I can assure you that it's not a great look.

As a designer—and as a person who appreciates order—my nightmare scenario is walking into someone's home and being hit with a collection right at the entryway. If it's the first thing you experience when you walk in, then the homeowner has taken his or her obsession entirely too far. I don't want to be greeted by fifteen colonial rag dolls, and I don't want to be so overwhelmed by your porcelain cat collection that I'm questioning whether I should take off my coat or run in the opposite direction.

If you're a collector, a good rule of thumb is to pick ten to fifteen favorite finds from your stash, then tastefully display just those. You don't have to part with the rest: instead, buy cabinets so that you can keep them organized, somewhere where they are easily accessible but out of sight. If you collect large pieces or have a significant amount of one thing that you absolutely can't bear to put away, it's best to sprinkle the items throughout your home in small doses so that your space is punctuated with the most meaningful objects. Don't pile a million knickknacks into one room or it will look like you live in a garage sale.

When I'm working with a client who values his or her collectibles, I try to think of them as pops of color and personality. If you have a muted room, your collection can be the cherry on top. Here are a few ways to maximize your treasures.

I collect ashtrays and glasses from various restaurants, hotels, and events I've been to and display them together alongside little handwritten notes to remind myself of where I got them. Looking at them immediately transports me back to these fun times.

make sense
of small objects

I've met so many people who have one type
of item that they like to pick up as a souvenir
whenever they find a chic new establishment
or go on vacation someplace they've
never been. Ashtrays are my own personal
keepsakes. There are a few gorgeous Hermès
ones I've received as gifts. I also collect
ashtrays when I visit a cool bar or restaurant,
and they become little mementos. My favorite
ones get displayed in my family room,
since that's a cozy space where guests tend to
congregate. When you have a lot of a little
things, strategically place them in an
area where they feel most relevant to the space
so that they become a conversation starter
when you entertain.

*When you have a large quantity of similar objects
in one collection, sorting and displaying them by color or theme
can help make the grouping feel cohesive and thoughtful.*

Homeowners often collect special holiday pieces that are displayed at certain times of year. In these instances, I like grouping similar items together for maximum impact—a table with beautiful candlesticks, or a stack of delicately wrapped packages.

be smart about barware

I love sipping a cocktail, but I really love
having a beautiful glass to drink it out of. It's
nice for my guests to have that experience
too. The beauty of hoarding glassware is that you
can actually use it. A formal dining room
looks so chic when the table is set for the season
with beautiful glasses—and you can quickly change
them out and give the tablescape an entirely
new look. When displaying glasses in cabinets or
on a bar, try arranging them so that the most
colorful ones are up front and the clear glasses are
toward the back. Group the colorful ones by
shade, or mix them up for a more eclectic look.

feature your favorite fashions

My absolute favorite items to hoard
are Fendi bags. They are like
pieces of jewelry because each one is
unique. I dream of hanging them
on hooks and making a grid on every
wall of my bedroom, but I have
no doubt that it would drive my husband
right out of the house. I generally
find that the best way to display special
designer pieces and fashion items
is to incorporate them into the closet
design. A lot of women want to see their
beautiful gowns every time they get
dressed, and if so, we'll create sections
of the closet with retractable poles
and hooks so that anything they love can
always be hanging in full view. The
same is true for menswear, including
tuxedos, jackets, and ties, so—when space
allows—it can be worthwhile to mount
a hook or bar for the special pieces to
hang on display. Generally, people appreciate
being able to view these items in a space
that is private and a little more personal.
Thankfully, I've never had anyone ask me to
put an Oscar de la Renta in the living room.

*When you invest in special pieces for
your wardrobe, they shouldn't be relegated
to a drawer or the back of your closet.
Whether you hoard shoes, bags, or various
vintage finds, put them on display so that you can
enjoy them each time you open the door.*

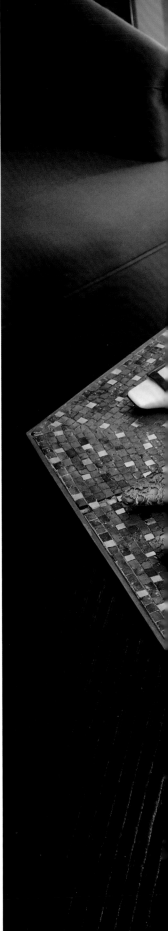

stock up on furniture

One surprisingly popular thing I've
seen people collect? Chairs. You can mix
and match them with different
accessories, and you can't have too
many. You can use them for dining or
at a desk; you can place them next
to a console or pair them with an armoire.
A fun mix of chairs is way more easily
managed than a giant collection of
movie posters. Chairs don't have to be a
big-ticket spend, plus they can help change
the look of a room when you move
them from place to place. When you're
having a party, no one is going to complain
about having an extra place to sit.

*The chairs that accent Jillian and Patrick Dempsey's
dining banquette can just as easily be moved into the living
room or formal dining room to accommodate
guests during a gathering. They are all different styles,
but they all serve a practical purpose.*

sort by meaning

As the amount of public attention
on crystal healing and gemstones grows,
so does the presence of these objects
in people's homes. I worked with
one client who had so many crystals of
all different sizes that it was a true
challenge to find ways of integrating
them into the decor. We ended up making
her fireplace into a little work of
art using the crystals. We put the largest
ones on the floor and the mantel, then
arranged the smaller ones on surrounding
shelves. Certain crystals support
romantic and loving intentions, so those
went in the master bedroom, whereas
other give off energy, so those were placed
near the front door. When items have
emotional, scientific, or historical
relevance, you can determine which room to
place them in based on their meaning.

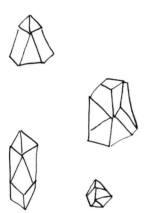

*One way to make a gallery wall look even more
impactful is to organize the images you're displaying
by event or by artist so that the wall tells a story
as the eye travels across it, a technique we used
to arrange the photos in Sophia Bush's home.*

Consider curating small groupings of collectibles and incorporating them into your table setting by theme or by color when you're entertaining. It's a way of putting favorite pieces front and center, and it also allows you to easily change the look and feel of your table.

savor wedding memories in small doses

Framing photos, mounting collages, and finding creative ways to display guest books and invitations are challenges that homeowners constantly struggle with. It's natural to feel obligated to make wedding memories prominent in your home, and displaying a beautiful picture or two can feel just right, but you don't need to wallpaper your house with your entire wedding album. Think of it this way: there's a good chance that any visitors to your living room were at your wedding too, so they don't need to relive the day when they come over for dinner. Trust me, I love weddings, so it's nothing against yours!

Incorporating a few framed family photos into a common area can be beautiful, especially when the photos are interspersed among other pieces of art, but if you want to display a significant number of wedding pictures or shots of your children, opt for a bedroom or den instead.

toilette

Crafting the perfect aesthetic in common areas like the living room, dining room, and guest rooms is often such a priority that other areas—the ones that see less foot traffic—get put on hold. Many homeowners and designers leave the bathroom design until the end of the project. As a small space, it often tends to be the last item on the checklist. But for me, it's one of the first spaces I want to dive into because I know I'll have an absolute blast with it. No matter how subdued a homeowner's taste, there's a little part of everyone that wants to get funky and let their fantasies run wild. You don't have to veer into a lane so dramatic that it would make Donatella Versace proud, but here's my advice: let yourself go a little crazy when you plan your bathroom. Because it's a more private part of the home and not a space where guests gather, it's okay for a bathroom to have a different vibe from the rest of the house—particularly a master bath, which is usually tucked away and serves as your own personal sanctuary.

a space to play

You spend so much time in the bathroom that it's nice to mix in special features, hardware touches, and materials that make you happy every time you're in there. A bathroom is like a Rubik's Cube because there are so many different combinations of extras that you can use on a small scale or a large one. No client would ever let me marble an entire living room, but if I find an incredible material that I want to deck out the bathroom with, it's a safe space to play in. While the seemingly limitless options are a designer's ecstasy, they can easily overwhelm a homeowner, particularly one who is doing a bathroom remodel on his or her own. Because bathrooms are typically tiny spaces, it's hard to grasp the scale of each individual element. Tiles and flooring look huge once placed, especially if you're going with a bold design, whereas fixtures are extremely small. Further complicating the selection process, these elements are typically sourced from a variety of vendors—people will see marble they like at one place, then a faucet they like at another, but those pieces may not make sense when you put them together.

Creating his-and-hers spaces is one of the most interesting opportunities to reflect the homeowners' different tastes. In one Los Angeles couple's home, her space, the master bath, is packed with super-colorful mosaics. It's vivid, it's playful, and everywhere you look, there is a bright treat for the eye. On the other hand, his bathroom is enviably peaceful and simple— all white materials with a floating antique marble sink and gorgeous, intricate spouts and shower fixtures. The two spaces couldn't be more opposite, and I love that they're in the same home because it highlights the complementary personalities of the couple. Keeping distinct aesthetics in separate spaces is a solid tactic even when you're doing a design project without the help of an interiors pro.

If you're not a professional, sourcing bathroom materials can be the drunk dial of home design. This isn't the time for Amazon Prime—you should go look at every material you want and get samples of everything so that you can envision it all together.

The bathroom in Hollywood's Petit Trois restaurant feels classically French, but with a vibrant splash of color. Chef Ludo Lefebvre often tells me that the tile is his favorite part of the design because it's so bold.

It's easy to fall into the trap of choosing bathroom details in a piecemeal way, but the key to making such a small space work is to ensure that all colors, finishes, and fixtures make sense together. If you're hesitant to do bold color in your bathroom, there are a variety of white tiles and marbles that can blend well with different types of hardware.

find your chill zone

I strive to create bathrooms that make you feel like you're staying in a gorgeous hotel. I don't want to come home at the end of the day to see tubes of toothpaste lying on the counter or damp towels thrown on the floor. Clutter exists—we all have it—but there are clever ways of hiding it when you craft a design.

RELY ON HOOKS

Homeowners always want towel bars installed, but for a guest bedroom, I prefer to fold towels and stack them in a cabinet so that they are out of sight and guests can grab a fresh one each time they shower. If you're going to mount something on the wall, robe hooks offer easy access to a gorgeous fluffy robe to slip into while getting ready. In a master bath, towel hooks are helpful.

MAKE VANITY CLUTTER VANISH

So many people keep bottles of fragrance, foundation, and lipsticks all over their countertops, but it makes the eyes focus on the clutter rather than the beautiful design of the space. Leave your vanity mellow by installing deep drawers where you can stash your daily essentials.

MINIMIZE YOUR MEDICINE CABINET

There's no doubt that medicine cabinets are practical, but they can be an eyesore if they protrude from the wall. If I come in at the beginning of a job, then I always try to install them so that the door is flush with the mirror or the wall. If the cabinet juts out, or if it's framed by molding, it breaks up your wall in such a way that your whole space seems smaller and more closed in. If you're moving in somewhere and are stuck with a medicine cabinet that isn't flush, keep the wall décor very minimal so that it doesn't make the space seem even more crowded.

DON'T NEGLECT YOUR SHOWER DOOR

The shower entrance is the forgotten child of bathroom design. So many people tile the inside of the shower but leave the surrounding area in drywall. I always tell my clients to give the entrance to their shower the same importance that they do the entrance to their home—it shouldn't be left alone. Consider surrounding the door with something that complements the interior of the shower, like stone or ceramic. Shower doors themselves have evolved in recent years, and the options now go far beyond simple glass doors on hinges. Brass and steel fittings make for incredibly chic shower doors. I also obsess over glass doors that are surrounded by metal trim with dividers at the top.

CHOOSE A LIGHT COLOR

Almost every single bathroom I've designed is painted white, a very light shade of gray, or a muted shade of pink, green, or blue. I've never done a dark bathroom because it can feel depressing. A bathroom should be clean and bright, with light bouncing off the walls to give everything a little extra sparkle. Since a bathroom is meant to be a functional space for bathing and primping, homeowners tend to avoid accessories that add personality. But it can be the perfect nook for a few accents that tie into the rest of your home, like sconce lighting or a framed memento—these small changes can have a big impact.

keeping the peace

A common mistake when it comes to making your bathroom a beauty is getting too carried away with details. It's crucial to pick a lane and stay in it. (Again, you don't want it to look like you pieced together your vanity and sink while six martinis deep.) I'm often asked to come into a client's home to fix mistakes made by previous owners. One house had seven bathrooms, and nothing within any of those bathrooms worked together. There were mismatched colors, different finishes, and hardware that didn't make any sense in combination. The design had gone too far in the eclectic direction, so all these rooms felt out of place in the context of the house. You don't have to merge all the way into the slow lane, but you should curb yourself before things start to feel random.

One of my all-time favorite bathrooms belongs to actress Sasha Alexander. She had serious buyer's remorse after she closed on her home. The master bath walls were sponge-painted in orange and red, and the old wood cabinets were warped so badly that they weren't usable. But we transformed it into a space so serene that it became Sasha's favorite room in the house. The final product featured very little color—it's all white with beautiful limestone countertops and bleached wood cabinets. It feels peaceful, luxe, and special, and it proves that you can do something unique and satisfying without going to an extreme. Think beyond subway tile and do something that's going to make you want to hang out in there beyond the time it takes you to shower and brush your teeth.

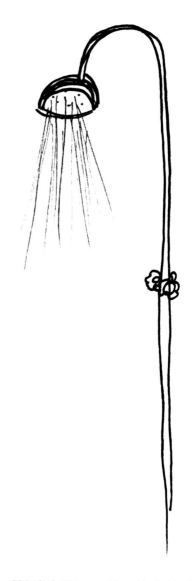

PREVIOUS: Wallpaper adds a whimsical touch to a space, so after meeting illustrator Carly Kuhn of The Cartorialist, I knew we had to partner to create something really special. In collaboration with interior designer Brigette Romanek, we created a made-to-order wallpaper collection featuring Carly's sketches—this "Mooner" print is perfect for the bathroom.
OPPOSITE: Sasha Alexander's Los Angeles master bath is one of my all-time favorite transformations. The goal was to make this space super tranquil and take it as far away from the orange-colored original as possible.

mary-kate olsen
interviews sasha alexander

MARY-KATE OLSEN Give me your best description of an Estee greeting.

SASHA ALEXANDER Her arrivals on site are always filled with enthusiasm, slight angst, and total creative charge.

MARY-KATE OLSEN What are some of the things you've disagreed on?

SASHA ALEXANDER She designed our first family home. The house was dark and needed light and furnishing to make the spaces warm and inviting. Estee did all that, but our biggest debates were about making sure the fabrics were kid friendly. She would say, "Well, don't let the kids sit there." I would say, "But it's a family room." She would say, "Well, too bad." That said, I don't make any decisions in my home without her input. Even choices I resisted initially, I eventually came around to know she was right. No one has her eye and sense for design.

MARY-KATE OLSEN Has Estee ever convinced you to totally blow your budget?

SASHA ALEXANDER She always sends multiple options for pieces at different price ranges. For example, her picks for chandeliers can range from $1,000 to maybe $100,000. Truth is, she wants to see me buy the $100,000 option knowing it was out of my budget. I would basically tell her to F-off, but I was left with the problem of not being able to imagine anything but that chandelier in the house. It drove me nuts. Her style and ideas are infectious.

MARY-KATE OLSEN Estee is famous for her sass . . . have you seen it in action?

SASHA ALEXANDER I do remember that she would speak to the male workers at the house with such an attitude that I would have to remind her they were working in my home and I didn't want them coming back to haunt me. Do you think she cared? Hell no. She couldn't stop herself. Whether it was a sarcastic comment about them not understanding what she wanted, or an eye roll, it's part of the fabric of her being. We love our Estee.

OPPOSITE: Combining various textures and finishes in the
walls, vanity area, flooring, and accessories can add dimension to
a room, particularly when a subtle pop of color is introduced.
ABOVE: A stunning shower door can elevate the look of the entire
bathroom. Here, the gleaming tiles are accented by a brass
door frame that suggests that the shower is an inviting, sectioned-off
oasis. PAGES 146–147: Turn your bathroom into a retreat for yourself
as well as overnight guests by adding special elements: a comfortable
chair, plush bath towels hanging near the tub, and shelves filled
with your favorite products for grooming and pampering.

inspiration

I often gravitate toward blues and greens in bathroom design, as these bright hues reflect light and
make the room feel clean and airy. I caution homeowners to stay away from dark bathrooms. After all,
it's where you groom yourself and get ready for the day, so you want to be able to see well!

layering

C reating a space that is equal parts functional, elevated, and personal requires experimenting with scale, blending the old with the new, and placing just as much emphasis on fine details and finishing touches as on the blueprint and construction. Infusing personality into a dwelling doesn't always necessitate a full architectural renovation. It can be as simple as strategically displaying the items that make a space feel lived-in rather than staged.

My favorite thing about my office space is the way I've casually amassed a family photo collage on the wall across from my desk, rather than behind it, so that I can look at it every day as I work and feel inspired. I can add to it whenever I want—it's a simple way of injecting life into an office.

Similarly, the decorative items in your home are an extension of your personality. What you are trying to communicate via art, photographs, and mementos is incredibly subjective. It's like buying a mattress—you should be the one to make the final decision on what works best for you. As your designer, I'll tell you what type of bed frame will look stunning in your master, but I'll never suggest whether you should go with a firm or a pillow-top mattress. In the same way, I can style all the accessories in a room, but I won't necessarily choose which photographs to frame or what paintings should be on display. I don't think of these extras as a part of the palette or the design—they live in their own world and can be added anywhere. You can have a minimal aesthetic for your design but totally eclectic art.

Whether it's a favorite piece of art, a seating solution, a stack of books, or a cluster of framed photos, a favorite find showcased in an entryway gives visitors an immediate sense of your style.

photographs

The gallery wall trend has made people much smarter about how to display photographs in an artful, planned-out way. Everyone is getting the memo that photos look better if they are organized. If you're sprinkling mismatched or kitschy picture frames all over your house, it will look disjointed, and your pictures won't draw much attention. Rather than place frames in every room of the house, designate a few areas where you can show off your pictures, and swap them in and out occasionally to create a fresh look. I love creating a small area that's dedicated to showcasing beautiful photos, like a full photo wall, or a cozy corner where frames are hung in a grid on opposite sides. This type of impactful display will make your guests stop and look at what's inside those frames—after all, you *did* pay a significant fee for that newborn photo shoot, or to restore your grandma's wedding portraits. Also think out of the box when placing statement photographs: the mantel is a classic spot that catches the eye, but a strong image on a kitchen wall can add interest to the space.

Homeowners often don't think to display art in the kitchen since it's meant to be a functional space for food prep, but I love hanging a piece of eye-catching art in that space. Just make sure that anything delicate is properly protected by a frame and placed far enough away from heat sources that you won't risk damage. PAGES 156–157: When selecting wall hangings and other finishing touches, think about the natural focal point in your room. In my Sagaponack living room, the fireplace tends to be the first thing visitors notice, so it was important to frame it with art and sconces that subtly highlight the design rather than detract from it.

wall hangings

I don't look at artwork as something that needs
to be color-coordinated with a space. You can have
a green and white room but blue and pink art—
that doesn't bother me one bit. I often find myself
designing a space where a client has very
specific taste in art; I may not understand the
vision at all, but I won't have a problem working
it into the final product. The subject matter
of your art should not be viewed as something that
needs to "match" but rather as its own entity
that showcases your taste. However, it's important
to think about the scale of art and how the size
can impact the vibe of a room. If you have a large
space that's feeling empty, hanging an oversized
painting, tapestry, or decal can immediately
change the look, and it's less permanent than, say,
a bright accent wall. On the flip side, if you love
a room in its current state but simply want to freshen
things up, a few small paintings could add new
interest without overtaking the overall aesthetic.

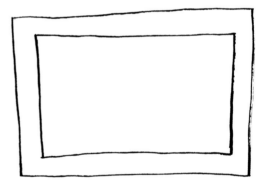

*Scale is more important than color and even subject
matter when it comes to art. Consider the dimensions of any
furniture you're hanging a painting above or beside to
ensure that it's not going to overwhelm its surroundings.*

Rather than a stand-alone centerpiece on a coffee table or end table, consider a grouping of like objects, such as vases, in various heights and forms.

light fixtures

The placement of light has a major impact on how a space looks. To supplement your permanent lighting solutions, like ceiling fixtures on dimmers, consider adding in lamps and sconces to areas that you want to illuminate or add dimension to in a nonpermanent way. As accent lighting is infused into a space, one thing that is often overlooked is the light bulb. There's a world of options when it comes to bulbs, and the standard soft whites that you can find at most drugstores are not the best-looking choice. If you have a lamp or a sconce where the bulb is visible, you want that to be just as gorgeous as the fixture it sits within. Look for a small round bulb that doesn't detract from the object itself. There are amazing teardrop shapes and exposed-filament bulbs that add a lust-worthy vintage touch—and you can find them at the nearest hardware store.

Never rush your bulb choice when installing a light fixture. The bulb itself should be as special and unique as the fixture it sits within.

worth the wait

Most clients' instinct is to hang art and display special objects immediately, in some cases even before furniture is selected. I understand the excitement and the urge to make your home feel as personal as possible, but I always push people to wait until the very end to add in decorative touches. You need to see all the elements of the space before you decide on the perfect place for an accent. I don't consider a home fully accessorized unless there's room for simple changes to be made long after I leave. I want to empower my clients to continuously reinvent without worrying that so much as moving a pillow or rearranging their framed pictures will turn their oasis into chaos.

Accessories are the easiest and most foolproof way to alter an aesthetic, and there's so much you can do on a small scale beyond replacing your pillows, throws, and decorative objects. Whether you're nearing the end of a major redesign or simply swapping out a few details to give your space a fresh look, these easy changes can have a big impact on the dynamic function of your home.

Art doesn't need to match the other items in a room. It can stand on its own as an element simply meant to reflect the personality and artistic sensibilities of the homeowner.

The key to styling an open-concept kitchen and dining room
is to display items in the same color family. Choose a tabletop that
complements the kitchen cabinets, and lighting fixtures with
similar tones. In this case, even your art choices should fall within the
same palette in order to convey an overarching vibe for the space.

moldings and doors

Because molding is made from wood, often
pine, it's relatively inexpensive to replace it for
a new look and feel. Changing out your flat
trim for chair rail molding can bring in texture
without requiring a major overhaul to any
room, and simply painting your white moldings a
darker shade can add dimension to a light space.
Staining raw molding can also create a
beautiful, rustic look. Similarly, if you're changing
over to dark moldings—and feeling ambitious
enough to extend the project a bit further—
consider painting your interior doors to match.
If you want to go even further, shake up an
exterior door. You walk through your front door
so many times each day, and entering your
home should make you feel inspired. A fresh coat
of a high-gloss, rustproof paint in a new color
is not only a quick fix for covering imperfections
but can also elevate the façade of your house.

A door is a passageway to your home, so don't neglect the façade.
A fresh coat of exterior paint, updated trim, or even strategically
placed shrubbery can completely refresh your entryway.

greenery

Plants enliven a space, and potted
arrangements beautifully punctuate any
palette. Infusing a bit of nature into
a room works for all tastes and aesthetics,
but only if you can commit to keeping
your plants alive. An amazing floor-
to-ceiling vine is not chic once it starts
to brown and ultimately keels over, but
air plants and topiaries are self-
sustaining options that require very
little maintenance and work well indoors.
If you travel often, pass on adding
a living thing to your home altogether.
As an alternative, I often incorporate
wallpaper printed with palm leaves or vines
to bring a natural feeling indoors.

*Plants add life to any room. Art that contains images of greenery is
a nice complement to—or even substitute for—the real deal.*

If you can keep a few plants alive, that's great. But regardless, you can consider other natural elements to bring a hint of the outdoors into your space. In Jillian and Patrick Dempsey's Los Angeles home, we found a beautiful way to stack wood for fueling the fireplace.

*Mirrors open up and enlarge a small room or even just a
dark nook or corner. Choose an interesting frame, and make sure
the space the mirror is reflecting is minimal and clean so that
you aren't shining a spotlight on clutter. If there's greenery or a
natural pattern to amplify through reflection, all the better.*

A porch or sunroom is the ultimate spot for bringing the natural elements of the outdoors inside. This sunroom in the Hamptons is accessorized with oversized planters, woven baskets, and rattan furnishings.

inspiration

A guest room is an ideal space for infusing fun or whimsical elements that will inspire those who stay there, like this hand-drawn wallpaper from our made-to-order collection with Carly Kuhn. When I know I want to use wallpaper or a particular print in a room, I'll start my mood board with that swatch, then slowly add in colors and textures that complement it.

minis

during both of my pregnancies, I spent hours searching for the perfect nursery accessories and carefully selecting pieces that I could imagine my babies growing up with. Most parents have a strong desire to nest, but it's amplified when you're an interior designer . . . by approximately one million percent. For my own children and for my clients, there's something magical about creating a space where you know little ones will play, learn, bond with their parents and siblings, and—if you're really lucky—sleep.

You might be tempted to make every single thing in a kiddie room adorable, but it's more practical to make the space adaptable so that it can grow with the child and the family. The room should feel youthful and tactile and inspire creativity but still reflect the overall composition of the home. I tend to avoid incorporating any elements that feel cartoonish, like baby wallpaper or campy character-themed decor. I never want guests walking through the home to say immediately, "Well, this must be the nursery." The connection to the homeowners' overall aesthetic should still be palpable.

My own style hasn't changed since I became a parent, and I don't believe that parents should sacrifice their taste, their lifestyle, and the home they've worked so hard to create once they have children. I'm very proud of the fact that my children, at only six and nine years old, are growing up to be incredibly respectful of what they're privileged to have. Not only does this attitude help preserve their toys, our furnishings, and our home overall, but I think it also teaches them that what they have is a result of how hard their parents have worked, and it motivates them to want to emulate those values in the future.

Designating spots for toys in bins or in a playhouse will make a child's room feel more organized and teach them where they have free rein to make a mess. The clubhouse in this room was meant to be a boy's own little space in which to let loose.

Just as your own bedroom is your sanctuary, your child's room should make you both feel at ease. Don't clutter surfaces with odds and ends—keep the space simple with practical accessories and just a few favorite toys on display.

growing gracefully

The bittersweet reality that all of us parents
must face is that the infant and toddler
years fly by faster than you can imagine. All
of my friends who have kids are in agreement
that the time and money you'll save by
creating rooms that will transition with each
phase of childhood are invaluable. That's why
you don't want to end up feeling stuck
with a design when a certain phase is over.
Furniture is an investment, so it's important
to think about the longevity of those
pieces. Couches can always transition, and
a sofa or loveseat is a nice touch for reading and
lounging with your kids and, later, as an extra
space for friends who sleep over. Bookcases
can also grow with a child. Shortly after
my daughter was born, I bought her an antique
bookcase from Paris, and six years later
it's still a perfect fit in her room. When she
was a baby, I propped it with plush stuffed
animals, now we use it to store her big
girl toys, and when she's older, we'll organize
her school textbooks on those shelves. Many
furniture companies make cribs that
convert into toddler beds, and then later into
full-size beds, and that's a smart investment
for parents to make. If you purchase a
traditional crib, you'll spend the next ten years
constantly upgrading your child's bed, and
increasing your carbon footprint in the process.

*PAGES 188–191: It's best to avoid any wall art
or murals that look cartoon-like, character-driven,
or particularly childish. Trust me—it will save you a paint
job in a few short years if you opt for something slightly more
elevated that will resonate just as much with a twelve-
year-old as it will with a toddler. Other ways to prolong the
design of a kids' space: Choose furniture made of
sturdy, durable materials that won't wear, and use recycled
materials for ottomans and throw pillows.*

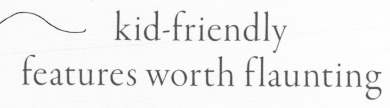

kid-friendly
features worth flaunting

When you have young children in your home, it's inevitable
that accidents will happen, no matter how much effort you put into teaching them the rules of the
house. During those critical years when any spot in the house can so easily turn into a
spill-prone zone, it pays to disaster-proof the high-traffic areas, like the kitchen and family room.

UPGRADE YOUR BABY GATES

Everyone goes to Target and gets the same
expandable gates for corralling toddlers and puppies,
and they tend to be an eyesore. Gates are necessary if
you have young kids or pets, but they shouldn't
be the one jarring element in an otherwise beautiful,
tranquil space. They can be custom made by your
contractor just as affordably with materials from the
hardware store. Simply follow these steps:

*Choose a shade and texture that matches either the wood of
your stairs or the material of your railing.*

*Measure carefully, and have your contractor secure
the material you choose and add the necessary fixtures to
safely attach it and allow it to open and close with ease.*

*Make sure that any rails or pallets are no more than
four inches apart to avoid any hazards with your tiniest
residents getting caught between the bars.*

*Count how much time you save on rushing around to hide
the old plastic gates every time you have company.*

*My favorite time-saver? Tell your significant other to
deal with this project.*

GIVE PRINTS A PURPOSE

Here's my rule of thumb for accent pieces, like
side chairs, throws, and pillows, that will be used in
family hangout spaces: prints are your best friend.
The busier the pattern, the more it will mask stains
caused by sticky hands and muddy mishaps. Trust
me—you'll have enough of those to deal with before
sending the little ones off to college.

USE FAUX LEATHER

When their little ones are still in the squirmy
stages, many parents have family dinners at the
kitchen table rather than in the formal dining
room. Faux leather is an inexpensive, durable option
for kitchen chair or banquette seat cushions—
it's a strong material that still looks sleek, and you
can easily wipe it down without worrying about
water damage. When I was designing Au Fudge, the
creative space for kids and adults in Los Angeles, I
pushed the envelope by using a lot of white, and this
material proved to be a successful solution.

REINVENT OLD RUGS

When an area rug reaches the point of needing to
be replaced, consider using a section of it to upholster
an ottoman for a family room or children's room.
This way if it gets trashed, it doesn't matter as much
since the fabric is old and not so precious to begin
with. If you can't avoid having little feet climbing on
an ottoman, at least you'll know that the material
on it was made to be walked all over.

timeless by design

I recently began redecorating my own house for the first time since my children were babies. Both of their rooms are almost the same as when my husband and I first designed them, which makes me feel good because the elements we chose stood the test of time. We never did anything too baby-friendly, like cartoon murals or quotes painted above their cribs. Now that I'm changing their rooms, my children are old enough to have opinions—my son even asked me to show him mood boards, which tells you a thing or two about whose child he is! When kids are old enough to care about their rooms and their belongings, they become mini hoarders faster than you can say Disney. Every corner of every room can easily be filled with primary-colored plastic playthings, which are an eyesore. In our house, we do a purge every three months to eliminate clutter. We sort what remains so that the kids know where to return their games, dolls, and activities when they're done playing with them. It's important to keep the clutter in check, not only for staying organized but also for your own mental health. Your home is your sanctuary—it should never be a place you want to escape.

Invest in furniture that will evolve with your children, not pieces that they will quickly outgrow. My daughter's room features dressers tand a bookshelf that she will have until college, as well as a comfy couch where we do a lot of reading and relaxing.

In designing West Hollywood's Au Fudge, my partners and I knew it would be subject to heavy wear and tear, so we used durable materials for the benches and chairs so they could easily be wiped clean. Consider brightly colored wood surfaces and sturdy faux leather for your kid-friendly spaces at home. You won't regret it.

inspiration

It's almost impossible to avoid the go-to pastel hues like pinks, blues, and purples for nurseries and children's rooms. The trick to making these shades work in a timeless way is to pair them with patterns and materials that feel elevated and grown-up.

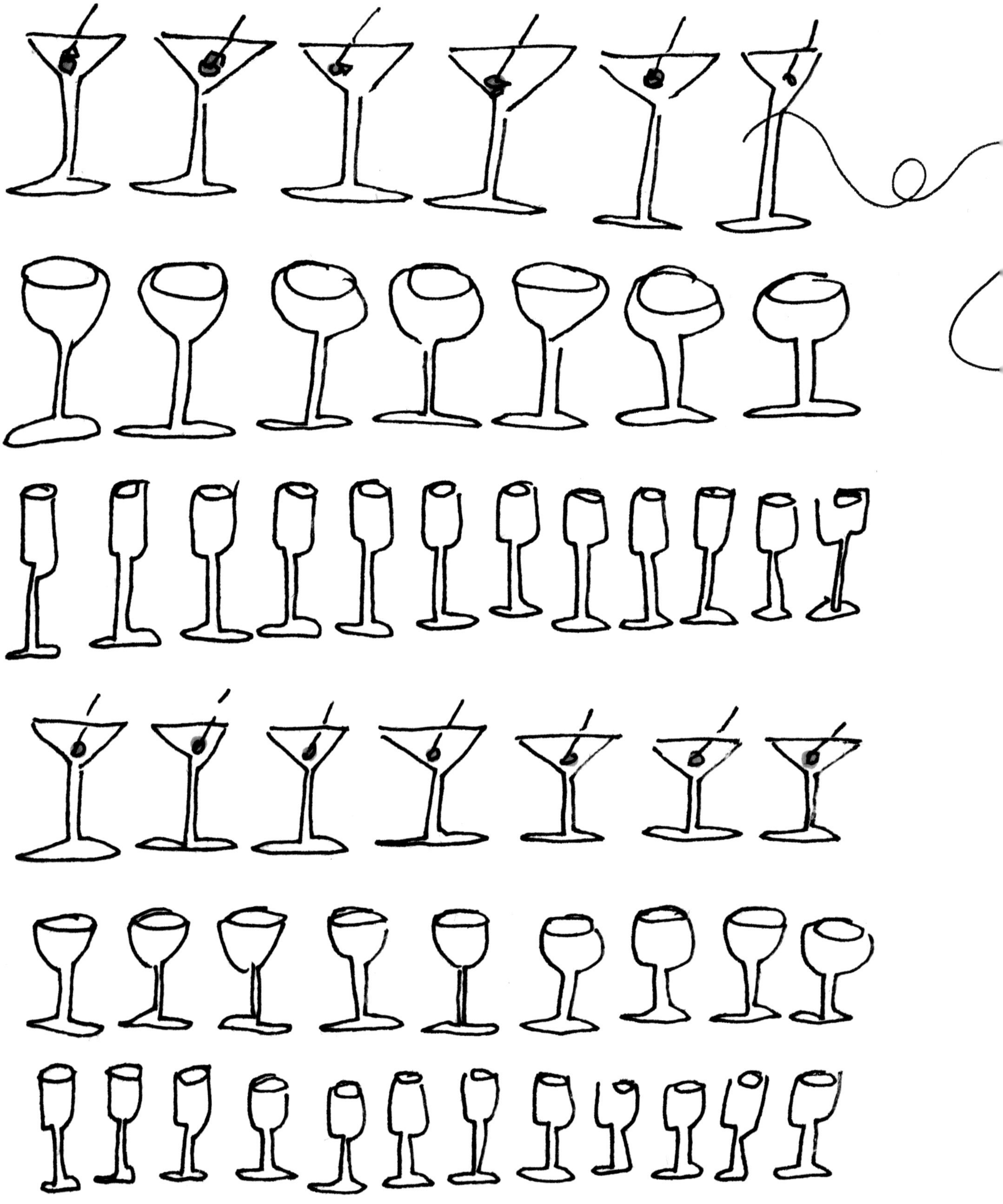

celebrating

as a little girl, when I watched my grandmother entertain every week, the thing that stood out the most to me wasn't how impeccably she put together each course or how clean her house was when the crowd arrived but rather how much she truly enjoyed those gatherings. Although she hosted week after week, she always put effort into making each party feel different. She mixed and matched her dishware and created elegant themes so that every event told its own unique story.

What was lost on me as a kid that I now appreciate is how important the parties were for the friendships of those who attended. The older you get and the busier life becomes, the harder it is to spend time with friends and truly savor those moments. Everything doesn't have to be perfect—it's more about showing guests how much you appreciate them and offering a little escape where they're taken care of and catered to for a few of hours.

If I didn't entertain as much as I do, I would hardly get to see some of the people in my life. If that makes my penchant for hosting selfish, then so be it. I love doing it, and I've lost count of all the people who have told me about new friendships they've forged at my parties over the years. Being in someone's home is so much more intimate and relaxing than going to a club or a restaurant, and a relaxed atmosphere lends itself to more mingling, deeper conversation, and closer personal connections. I'm like a kid getting ready for my birthday party when I plan my soirées—you never know what the night might bring.

When you have people over to your home, no area should be "off-limits" for friends to gather. A small dining nook in the kitchen can be just as much a space for guests to sit and chat as a formal dining room is.

thoughtful details

Whenever I throw a party, the first thing I take into consideration is how much effort my guests will put in just to be there. By the time they've set foot in my house, most people have already arranged for a babysitter, picked up a bottle of wine or another hostess gift, and paid for an Uber. The least I can do is impress them when they get here. I was recently at a party that I dropped a hundred dollars on a babysitter and a ride to attend only to spend the night eating chips and drinking out of a red plastic cup. On the contrary, it's so lovely, warm, and inviting when you see that your host has taken the time to prepare handmade place cards for every guest at a dinner party. In fact, I save these mementos and display them in a case in my own home as a reminder of the good times.

When I host, I obsess over the tiniest details because I think the biggest mistake that people make is not overthinking the elements of a night that will stand out to their guests. Rather than shoot off a text message with the party details, I like to prepare an invitation on Paperless Post. You can choose a design that matches the theme of your party, and it's easy to manage the guest list so that you aren't frantically following up to get a final head count. It never hurts to enlist a housekeeper to come the day before the party to make sure everything looks crisp and clean. I'll drive to the flower market as soon as it opens the morning of the party so that I can get the freshest blooms to display— not only do they look more unique than what you'll find at a florist, you can also tailor arrangements to what you know your guests love. Candles are displayed in each room and lit about twenty minutes before guests arrive so that the whole house smells enticing. My vintage wineglasses serve as vessels for a signature cocktail. (My Greyhound never disappoints—just mix equal parts fresh grapefruit juice, vodka, and Perrier.) I take out my good china, even when we're just having pizza and passed appetizers. If you registered for the fancy stuff only to let it sit in a cabinet while your dearest friends eat off paper plates, then you're not partying to your fullest potential.

A table setting allows you to mix and match
easily to achieve a fresh look each time you entertain.
A graphic placemat is the perfect backdrop for
earth-toned dishes and serveware.

take a shortcut

Sometimes the best way to take care of your guests
is to leave yourself enough time to mingle during the main event. I never cut corners when
it comes to making sure I can have a great conversation and a few laughs with
everyone in my home. I employ these party hacks so I can spend more time making
memories and less time making a mess of my kitchen.

PREMADE SNACKS

You don't have to cook something from scratch to please a crowd. There's nothing wrong with offering the comfort foods that we all crave and dressing them up in beautiful serveware. Trader Joe's has the best hummus ever, so I'll scoop it into a pretty bowl and garnish it with nuts. I've also ordered thin-crust pizza from a local eatery, cut it up into small squares, and set it on an antique tray for people to nibble on during cocktails.

DISPOSABLE DISHWARE

If I'm hosting a very big crowd, I'll buy disposable plates and cups without compromising on style or design. Meri Meri is an online company that specializes in children's parties, but some of the designs are so elevated that I'll often use the printed appetizer plates for adult hangouts. Recycled bamboo plates and utensils can look really chic for an outdoor affair. If my guest list outnumbers my fine glassware, I order plastic Berevino stemless wineglasses on Amazon in bulk. They're shatterproof, so they feel sturdy, and they look just like the real deal.

STANDBY BAR MENU

Consider hiring a bartender to come an hour before guests arrive and set up an area for drinks and dishware so everything is in one easily accessible place. It's a nice touch for people to be served, and it's easier on the host not to have to run around on refill duty. I have go-to wine selections that I stock up on regularly; that way, I never have to frantically look for recommendations before a gathering. If I'm hosting a huge crowd, I serve Whispering Angel and Miraval rosés and Flowers Pinot Noir. If it's a more intimate gathering, I love MiP rosé, François Crochet Sancerre rosé, and Sea Smoke Pinot Noir.

KIDS' ENTERTAINMENT

As refreshing as it is to have an adults-only night, so many friends have young kids that I'll often invite the whole family and plan an activity for the tots while the parents relax uninterrupted. A movie is the best way to keep a crowd of kiddos all occupied at once and minimize running, screaming, and party-crashing.

Keeping the surface of your table minimal allows it
to be a clean backdrop for mixing and matching
dish and glassware combinations so you aren't limited
to working within sets of a particular style.

PREVIOUS: More is more when it comes to incorporating fresh blooms into your place setting, particularly if your table or dining set features a raw wood finish that perfectly meshes with nature. OPPOSITE: Glassware shouldn't be relegated to kitchen cabinets—or, worse, storage boxes in an attic or garage—until your next big event. Make an impact by grouping similar silhouettes and displaying them on shelving or in a display case or an open-front cabinet.

inspiration Preparing your space for holiday entertaining gives you the flexibility to go over-the-top with colors, patterns, and the extra details that help get guests in the spirit of the season. Consider deep hues and cozy textures. Even temporary elements, like wrapped gifts on display, can speak to your seasonal inspiration while they last!

the petit trois touch
with ludovic lefebvre and jessica biel

ESTEE When my friends get together, the conversation often turns to food. Because I entertain so frequently, the home space and irresistible cuisine have always been intertwined in my world. For years I dreamed of designing a commercial restaurant space, and finally got the chance when I partnered with chef Ludo Lefebvre on his delectable Los Angeles restaurant Petit Trois in 2014. Two years later, I opened Au Fudge in West Hollywood with my friend, client, and co-owner Jessica Biel. After Ludo and I prepared for the opening of Petit Trois's second location in Sherman Oaks, Jessica sat down with us to discuss French style, blending the masculine with the feminine, and learning to live without those totally impractical dream items topping your lust list.

JESSICA What was the inspiration for the original Petit Trois design?

ESTEE Ludo envisioned a traditional Parisian eatery. He kept not-so-subtly reminding me that I knew nothing about French culture, so my mission was to prove him wrong. He would go so far as to joke that I had never even been to Paris!

LUDO My torture techniques must have worked given how beautiful the restaurant turned out. I wanted the interior of the restaurant to emulate French lifestyle in that it would not only be a place you could go for quality food, but also to meet people and enjoy the ambience. The tables are purposefully close together so that people can casually talk. I think this charm is the reason we've been successful—you're not just eating out; you're engaging in a social activity. All I need is a rude staff so that we can feel like we are in France!

JESSICA Why did you decide to hire Estee?

LUDO I researched her past work, and I saw that Estee hadn't designed a lot of restaurants. It was important to me that she hadn't because I wanted Petit Trois to be different. By hiring a designer who is so talented in the residential space, I knew she would bring something unusual to the table. After all, I wanted people to come in not only for the food but also for the design.

JESSICA Did you ever come close to firing her? I hear that you had a few spats . . .

LUDO We disagreed about a lot of things because I'm French and I think I know everything. But, as it turns out, I'm not an interior designer and that's why I hired Estee. I had to keep reminding myself of that.

ESTEE I don't tell you what to make when you come over to cook for my parties!

LUDO When Estee designs a space, she understands what's functional. It's so important to have function in a house, and even more important in a commercial space.

JESSICA How did you consider the menu in relation to the decor at Petit Trois?

LUDO Ah, this is where Estee and I come together. My menu is very classic, but although I don't change my recipes and flavors very often, I do change the techniques I use to achieve them. I think Estee's design process is similar. She does very clean, classic spaces, but each one has an unexpected twist, like the dark wood accents against patterned wallpaper in the restaurant. I was so worried that it would make the restaurant look dark, but when I walked in and saw it I was amazed. It's incredibly simple but it has a large impact.

ESTEE I like to blend both masculine and feminine details in the same room so that the aesthetic doesn't lean too far in one direction. The print of that wallpaper is very feminine, but the colors are not. The dark wood in the restaurant is masculine, but the marble detailing is not.

JESSICA How did you think about infusing color when designing the original Petit Trois?

LUDO Color and texture are just as important in interiors as they are when you're creating a dish. It's the first impression so it's important what feelings they evoke. I wanted to incorporate green into Petit Trois because it reminds me of the French countryside. Our bathroom is tiled in green and it's one of my favorite rooms to look at.

ESTEE In the new Petit Trois in the Valley, we're incorporating even more green because it's Ludo's favorite thing. The challenge for me was finding different versions of the color and mixing it in various shades. We thought about doing some dark browns and working within this classic French color scheme, but we ultimately decided that we wanted to modernize the palette a bit. We went with rich greens against black wood, which is super sexy and modern.

JESSICA What do you think is the secret to great style? Ludo, you talk about being "traditionally French," and I think that's always in style.

LUDO I would say that in both fashion and interiors, you can't go wrong with black and white, and I like the ease of that idea. When in doubt, choose black and white. So many of the details that we incorporated into the original Petit Trois will never go out of style because of that. We can look back at it in ten years and it will still be beautiful. It's not trendy or of-the-moment. It's simple and elegant.

ESTEE Jessica, even when I was styling you for the red carpet, I applied the same principle. There aren't many of your looks that we would think back and wonder, "Why did we do that?"

JESSICA It's true! Ludo, how else does Estee leave her mark on a room or a space? What makes up that special magic dust that she sprinkles everywhere?

LUDO Good energy! Estee and I had never met before working on Petit Trois and the one thing that marked the project was the positivity and creativity she brought with her. You have a formula, Estee, and after working with you, I can look at a space and know that it was you who designed it.

JESSICA I always say that Estee masters the combination of being super elegant and completely irreverent. She'll mix insanely gorgeous luxury objects with tiny little trinkets that are completely ridiculous—and sometimes even stolen! That's the mix of you, Estee.

ESTEE Some rules should be broken, and I never want to take myself too seriously. I just want to create a space that looks beautiful and makes you want to let loose and have a good time.

JESSICA What do you both splurge on when you go out?

ESTEE Alcohol. I love a fancy drink.

LUDO Good wine. I don't drink very often, but when I do, I want it to be something delicious that I'm sipping. I also spend more on meat. I eat less and less of it, but when I do indulge, I would rather have the best cut of steak possible.

JESSICA If you were a cocktail, what would you be?

LUDO I would be a Negroni because I love citrus and Campari.

ESTEE I would be champagne . . . rosé champagne.

JESSICA What's your favorite kind of party to throw?

ESTEE The kind where Ludo comes over to cook for me. He's my secret ingredient, and I don't like to share him.

LUDO I love hosting a barbeque. It's the type of party where I don't have to do too much, so I can spend time with my guests. I'll grill crab with butter and make a big pot of rice. I line a table with newspaper, put the crab in the middle, and offer Japanese mayonnaise, butter, and seaweed to garnish. It's a fun, casual way to host families and kids . . . everyone can share.

JESSICA What's the most impressive thing you can serve in a pinch?

LUDO Good-quality bread, cheese, and butter. If you can turn those into a grilled cheese, even better.

JESSICA Where is the strangest place you've found inspiration for your work?

ESTEE The Crazy Horse cabaret in Paris. It's a true production and such a beautiful presentation of color, lights, and ambience everywhere you turn.

JESSICA Were there any elements that you were so inspired to include in the Petit Trois design, but ultimately didn't?

LUDO It's a challenge to ask a designer to create a beautiful, impactful space, but also work within a strict budget.

ESTEE Shortly after we started Petit Trois, the space next door became available, so it was added on and has become the private dining room. I wanted to do different seating in that room because it was smaller, so I found gorgeous Italian palm-printed chairs that I fell in love with . . . but they were outside of our budget.

LUDO Estee and I almost divorced over these chairs. It was too much of a risk that they would get destroyed in a restaurant, where people are constantly in and out, especially when we try to be child-friendly. Every time we decided no, Estee came back with the same chairs and a different idea for where to put them.

ESTEE I'm relentless. I still think we should order at least one so that I can to sit in it when I come. I'll send you the invoice.

The design for Petit Trois Valley features a blend of masculine and feminine elements, like bold geometric tiles and a subtle floral wallpaper, that make the dining room feel classically French.

exteriors

When you open your home to friends, it's crucial to think about how each corner, nook, and bay can be inviting—both indoors and out. Of course, it will only enhance your own enjoyment of your home too. I never fully utilized the outdoor space at the front of my house during parties until recently, after I made an incredibly minor change: I lacquered and reupholstered a bench and several chairs there. Something as simple as rethinking a few seating options totally transformed my front patio into an appealing hangout area. This spot is situated right outside the French doors that lead into my smoking room, so it has become a cool little alcove where guests can lounge during parties.

Regardless of whether a property is large or small, I like to think of any outdoor space as an extension of the house. Often, the instinct is to set up one sitting area with a table, chairs, and a barbeque, then dedicate the rest of the property to landscaping. But it can be limiting to think of your patio as the only space for "living" outside, so I encourage my clients to view their property as one large room. The challenge? Dividing this giant open-air "room" into several small nooks, and giving each section a different purpose.

The secret to ensuring that your outdoor space is fully utilized is to place seating in areas that tend to be sparse so you and your guests are encouraged to sit down and take advantage.

the fun in functional

Because you don't have to worry about the boundaries of walls and ceilings in a yard, you can get creative with fewer limitations. Do a drawing of your space and split it up into areas based on your interests—sketching an outdoor space doesn't require architectural skills. If you love to grill, make a barbeque area that feels extra special. Place your barbeque close to the house so that you can easily access the indoor kitchen, and consider the climate you live in. If it's warm year-round, you may want to invest in a built-in barbecue unit that includes a refrigerator and freezer with a space for storing ice. If you live in a climate where you can only use the yard during three or four months of the year, then a stand-alone grill that you can easily store in the off-season may be the best choice.

If you love to entertain, think about how you can make your guests as comfortable as possible while dining alfresco. Instead of a traditional patio table, invest in outdoor couches surrounding an oversized coffee table, which should be arranged underneath a shaded area—no one wants to sweat while eating. If you have a large space, it will likely be worthwhile to supplement with additional outdoor seating, like picnic tables. My trick for creating a personalized seating space? Order a few standard wooden picnic tables online (you can find options for under three hundred dollars, and they fold up flat to store), then paint them different colors using boat paint. Marine-safe finishes will protect your tables from the elements and from getting scratched up by dishware and rogue Frisbees. We did a picnic-table setup at Au Fudge, and it lends a vibrant, whimsical touch.

Make the most of the fact that you're less limited by the dimensions of the space when designing a patio or yard. Go for those oversized chairs; you won't have to worry about them looking too large or overwhelming a room.

take the plunge

When starting a new outdoor project, the first thing to consider is the placement
of the pool. If the home has an existing pool, its shape and size inform where everything else will be placed.
If there isn't a pool, your first step should be to decide if you will add one. Customizing a pool from
the very infant stages is a thrill—sometimes quite literally. Two of my daredevil friends, Justin Timberlake
and Jessica Biel, once told me they wanted to be able to jump from a main heated pool into a smaller
cold-water pool. I came back to them with sketches featuring a twelve-inch step where you could dip your feet into
a wading pool, and they laughed out loud. Their pool is built into a hill, and they wanted to dive twelve
feet into a lower one. We did it, and every time I go to their house, they inevitably ask me to take the plunge—
and every time, I tell them no. For those of us who prefer to sit near the edge rather than live on it,
here are some considerations for a relaxing and safe wading experience.

NONSLIP SURFACES

People often go barefoot outside, so be mindful
of the surface of any stone or rock material
you're using for a patio or deck and avoid anything
that could be a slipping hazard when wet. Wood
decking and brick are optimal choices, whereas
limestone requires extra precautions. If you love
the look of stone, work with your contractor or
supplier to ensure that the limestone is honed to
improve traction, or consider options like sandstone,
slate, or granite. If you're not breaking ground,
Slip Grip is a solution for preexisting slippery
surfaces. They make a pool and spa line of products
that can be applied using a grout sponge—it
coats the surface and adds texture.

SAFETY GATES

Many communities require backyard pools to be
gated, but even if yours does not, it's essential
if you have children in your home. I've seen many
friends and clients do a DIY job with inexpensive
materials from the hardware store thinking
it will be a temporary solution until their little
ones grow up. But if you choose a luxe material,
you can build a proper gate that looks like
an integral part of your yard design. Wood and
wrought iron can be incredibly sleek and will last
for years with little maintenance.

TILING

There's nothing as refreshingly inviting as
bright blue, crystal clear water. White plaster on
the bottom and walls of your pool with a light
water-line tile is the best way to make your guests
want to take a dip. I tend to avoid designing
dark pools, but that may just be because
Jaws ruined me years ago when I first watched
it as a child.

SURROUNDING PATIO

The immediate area surrounding the pool
shouldn't be used for dining. Place your table and
chairs outside of the splash zone and leave a
buffer in between. If your ideal day of relaxation
includes lounging with a good book, section
off a portion of your pool deck or yard that
gets both sun and shade and insert plush daybeds,
hammocks, and end tables where you can rest
your essentials.

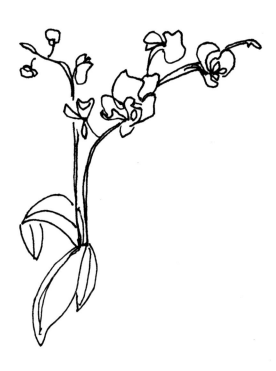

PREVIOUS: If you have a pool or plan to install one, plan the rest of the yard around that element. Don't finalize your patio design, lawn, or kids' play area until you finalize the pool design to ensure that you have adequate room for everything else to be functional. LEFT: Many homeowners are challenged by where to situate an outdoor dining area. More important than proximity to the house is where your table will be in relation to the pool, if you have one. It's better to have to walk a bit farther from your kitchen than to risk soggy entrées.

display the fun

Inside the home, it's always best to store
your games on shelves or in cabinets
to cut down on clutter, but your outdoor
space is where you can put the fun
stuff on display. I'm currently designing
a property that has a tennis court and
a bocce court, but many other clients
request smaller gaming accessories, like
outdoor Ping-Pong or billiard tables.
If you have a large deck or a wide-open
grass or gravel space, places to play
make great additions. In all my years
of designing, only one client has
asked me to build a grotto—but that's
a *whole* different kind of party.

*PREVIOUS: If you do prefer a seating area directly
poolside, make it a space for comfy chaise longues and
outdoor sofas rather than dining furniture. OPPOSITE:
Landscape design should relate to the style of your house.
Ensure that this element of your property complements
the exterior of your home. Also, consider the
placement of your windows in relation to where plants,
flowers, and shrubbery are or will be placed so you
can enjoy the view from indoors.*

Entertaining alfresco can be done on a large scale, with a full-size dining table set up outdoors (above), or on a much smaller scale, with a small nook suited for enjoying a cup of coffee or a cocktail with one or two guests (right).

*The placement of the pool, the oversized
planters, and the patio furniture creates an inviting
symmetry. Together these elements frame the
house in the most desirable way.*

inspiration

Pulling together swatches for outdoor spaces, patios, and sunrooms often means that I'll go a little brighter with colors and prints, particularly florals and stripes.

appendix

You've kid-proofed your fabrics and safeguarded your yard from slips and splash damage, but there are plenty of other measures you can take to preserve the tranquil and no-fuss vibes in your home. I recently walked into my house to find my husband on the top rung of a ladder and the globe from one of my all-time-favorite vintage light fixtures in a million pieces on the floor. His sweet intentions of repairing the globe had backfired, and while he thankfully emerged unscathed, you can't exactly replace unique vintage finds. Lighting repair is one of those pesky details on my list of "Things You Think You Know How to Do But Should Most Definitely Call a Professional For." Or, at the very least, enlist the help of a family member or neighbor so that you aren't putting yourself or your home at risk for the sake of completing a project. For a designer, the final stage of a project is the install—it's the icing on the cake of a home renovation. This is the part of the process where we take months' worth of blueprints, renderings, furniture orders, and contractor coordination and put it all together in your home. It's the coming to life of our joint vision. The finishing touches are deceptively tricky because they often seem like the "easy" parts. Installing a lightbulb, ordering furniture, or patching a wall can quickly escalate from manageable to chaotic if you don't plan properly. Here's what you should anticipate to avoid a late-game fail.

TAKE PROPER MEASUREMENTS Everyone loves Restoration Hardware's modular couches, but few people measure properly in order to ensure that the dimensions will work in their space. I had a client who measured his front entryway (perfect fit) but not his bedroom door (epic fail) and ultimately had to return the piece. A common misconception is that the length of a doorframe is the key measurement, but it's equally important to document the width. If the width of a door doesn't accommodate the depth of a couch or chair, you likely won't be able to jiggle it all the way through. It's also crucial to measure the space between all the furniture pieces in your room so that you don't end up with a sofa squeezed so close to your coffee table that you can't even stretch out your legs.

AVOID ONLINE SPLURGES If you're not working with an interiors professional, shopping online for large key pieces is not a strategic move. It requires the shopper to be very well-versed in fabrics and dimensions to fully understand how a piece will look and feel. Instead, go to a store so that you can touch everything . . . sit on the couches you're considering and get a sense of how vibrant the colors of a rug actually look. Ask for fabric samples of your favorites so that you can bring them to other vendors and coordinate your picks. You should feel completely at ease with everything in your house so that you don't find yourself having to ship a couch back on move-in day.

MAKE WALLPAPER SEAMLESS If you plan to wallpaper a room, first apply a coat of paint that matches the base shade of the paper. Many people assume that there's no need to touch the existing walls if they'll simply be covered by wallpaper, but it's extremely difficult to match up the seams of the paper. If the seam is even the slightest bit off, the original paint will peek through, which will be particularly glaring if your wallpaper is dark. Plan ahead since, unfortunately, this problem won't be apparent until you are far enough into the project that a significant amount of paper will already be glued to your walls.

PUT EFFORT INTO TOUCH-UPS It's common practice (and a good one) to roll on at least one coat of primer before you paint a room, particularly if you're shifting from a dark paint to a light one. But where many homeowners stray in the painting world is during touch-ups. If you're patch repairing a small dent or the hole where a picture frame was previously hung, it won't suffice to simply prime and paint the small affected area. Once that paint dries, it will be a slightly different shade and texture than the rest of the wall, particularly when the light hits it. Although priming and repainting the full wall takes longer and there is no instant gratification, take the time to do it right and avoid an eyesore in one spot.

GIVE YOURSELF—AND YOUR WALLS— A BREAK There is a very precise art to moving furniture in such a way that it doesn't damage your floors or your walls—or your back. Even with multiple people helping to push and pull, the most cumbersome pieces can still scratch wood and tile, rip off drywall, and break glass. Stock up on small felt furniture sliders that you can slip under each leg of a large piece to place your gorgeous finds right where they belong—no lifting required. When you're bringing in new furniture for the first time, leave it to the pros, who know how to maneuver your finds in and out of vehicles and through your home without damaging new fabrics or dragging elements of the outdoors in.

style file

If I could make a career out of spending hours on the internet discovering inspiring new resources, I would do it in a heartbeat. Ideally, I'd be on my couch with a glass of wine while searching for home accents, antiques, and objets d'art. The bookmarks tab on my browser is endless, and I am always on the lookout for the next best thing for my own home and for my clients. Here's the not-so-short list of my all-time favorite retailers, rental companies, and dreamy sites to browse.

1STDIBS (1stdibs.com)

This online marketplace connects you with the best antique dealers, gallery owners, and designers worldwide. All sellers are professionally vetted, so you never have to worry about quality.

APPARATUS

(apparatusstudio.com)

The New York–based Apparatus Studio has stunning, sculptural lighting made using materials like lacquer, porcelain, marble, and suede with chic brass accents. These pieces are so elevated that they could easily be in a museum.

ATELIER DE TROUPE

(atelierdetroupe.com)

"A de T," as it's known by the interiors crowd, has gorgeous sconces and accent pieces like unique chairs and end tables. They offer made-to-measure products, but you can also shop their ready-to-ship selection online.

BELLACOR (bellacor.com)

Bellacor is my go-to source for affordable outdoor lighting options, like wall mounts and string lights. You'll find plenty of cute under-$100 options here.

BENJAMIN MOORE

(benjaminmoore.com)

There's a reason everyone uses their paint—the colors are rich and saturated and the quality will last years.

BLACKMAN CRUZ (blackmancruz.com)

I'm obsessed with the eclectic mix of furniture and art Blackman Cruz offers—no two pieces are the same, and the items are sourced from all over the world. If you're in the Los Angeles area, the showroom is worth a visit—housed in a former nightclub, it's a supercool space.

BRENDA ANTIN (323-934-8451)

I've been incorporating chairs from Brenda's Los Angeles boutique into my designs for years. Her space is a treasure trove of antiques and collectibles. Some pieces I don't change one bit, and others are perfect candidates for updating and modernizing to become exactly what a client is looking for.

COLEEN & COMPANY

(coleenandcompany.com)

Coleen & Company does amazingly unique, colorful lighting. If you need a bright fuchsia wall sconce or an insanely whimsical chandelier, you'll find something perfect here.

COMPAS STONE AND TILE DESIGN

(compasstone.net)

For standout marble, stone flooring, French limestone, and terra cotta, I work with Compas. This is my spot when I'm looking to do a completely unique fireplace design.

CONSORT (consort-design.com)

Accent pieces are like jewelry for your home, and Consort has really unique finds. Their pricing runs the gamut, so you can find something incredible whether you're looking to spend fifty bucks or five thousand.

COWTAN & TOUT (cowtan.com)

My fabric secret, Cowtan & Tout has an endless library of materials that you can scroll through for inspiration. Just remember that a virtual swatch will never do a fabric justice, so you need to see and touch samples before making a selection.

DOMINGUE FINISHES

(www.dominguefinishes.com)

Domingue is one of my newest obsessions. They make incredible materials—like lime washes, mineral paints, and plasters—that give your home an insanely unique look. Plus, they've worked on actual royal palaces— you know, in case you need a reference.

FARROW AND BALL (us.farrow-ball.com)

With a palette of only 132 color options, Farrow & Ball obsesses over getting their pigments and finishes exactly right. Their colors are so deep and rich that they will instantly transform your space.

GARDE (gardeshop.com)
Garde offers a quirky mix of furnishings and accessories from both new and emerging designers. You can find a super established name and also discover someone you've never even heard of.

GEARYS (gearys.com)
I love displaying gorgeous serveware in my dining room *and* actually using it when I entertain. Geary's has fabulous fine china and silverware. You can also find special housewarming gifts here.

THE GOLDEN TRIANGLE
(goldentriangle.biz)
Home to an eclectic mix of Asian and European antiques, artifacts, lighting, and accessories, the Golden Triangle's 18,000-square-foot space is set up as mini vignettes that showcase these special finds.

HARBINGER (harbingerla.com/home)
Harbinger has the most awesome prints in everything from rugs to wallpaper to textiles. When I want to add a bold statement in a space, I look here.

JF CHEN (jfchen.com)
The antique studio JF Chen is a Hollywood secret . . . they have such a huge and gorgeous selection that it's become a source for directors and set designers over the years.

KALON (kalonstudios.com)
Because Kalon is known for simple, functional furniture that is also really durable, I often look for pieces to use in kids' rooms here.

LARSEN (larsenfabrics.com)
Manufacturing fabrics since the 1930s, Larsen has the widest assortment of prints. Their website has a "moodboard" feature where you can save your favorites as you map out your space.

LAWRENCE OF LA BREA
(lawrenceoflabrea.com)
Lawrence of La Brea has an insanely large selection of rugs that can fit any space. Bonus: they also have rental and cleaning services.

LUCCA ANTIQUES (luccaantiques.com)
I can guarantee that no matter the size or scale you're looking for, you can source antique lighting, seating, tables, and decor from Lucca.

MAISONETTE (maisonette.com)
The amount of time I spend getting completely lost in kids' websites is absurd. Maisonette has great wall hangings and bedding for kiddos, and an incredible selection of clothing and toys.

MERCI (merci-merci.com/en/)
The founders of children's fashion label Bonpoint opened Merci in the heart of Paris's Haut Marais historic district to bring together the worlds of fashion, design, and home goods. Where else can you find shelving units, gardening accessories, and designer watches in one place?

OLDE GOOD THINGS (ogtstore.com)
Olde Good Things sources unique architectural antiques, like doorknobs, decorative iron, and hardware. The team there also takes reclaimed materials and makes them into cool mirrors and accent pieces.

OLD WORLD WEAVERS (212-752-9000)
At East Coast fabric wholesaler Old World Weavers, I often find the materials to give a chair or a couch new life.

PAVILION ANTIQUES
(pavilionantiques.com)
The owners of the Chicago boutique Pavilion Antiques take frequent trips to France and Italy to source items that aren't easily found in the United States, then make them available to ship domestically. They always find the most stunning postwar pieces.

PETIT PAN (petitpan.com)
You'll find everything you could possibly need for *bébé* in the scrumptious Parisian shop Petit Pan, including handmade mobiles, pajama sets, and the sweetest printed pillows, blankets, and sheets.

PORTOLA PAINTS & GLAZES
(portolapaints.com)
Small batch paints made locally in Los Angeles allow you to create custom blends tailored perfectly to your decor style. The owners also design the most beautiful graphic wallpaper.

ROGERS + GOFFIGON (rogersandgoffigon.com)
One of the top producers of home furnishing textiles in the world, Rogers + Goffigon sources materials from family-owned European mills in a variety of textures, weights, and fibers.

SUMMIT (summitfurniture.com)
Summit's patio furniture is so beautiful—this is my favorite spot for finding outdoor pieces. Your backyard should be an extension of your space, so skip the plastic chairs and invest in a gorgeous wooden chaise.

TAI PING (houseoftaiping.com)
Tai Ping does everything bespoke, so it's great for custom fitting a totally unique design to your space.

THE FUTURE PERFECT
(thefutureperfect.com)
If you love contemporary design, then the Future Perfect is for you. They offer both studio-created works and one-of-a-kind pieces.

THE RUG COMPANY
(therugcompany.com)
With modern design and top-notch quality, The Rug Company offers a custom and bespoke service where you can work with the pros to create a unique piece tailored to the specifications of your home.

THE TOT (thetot.com/)
Not only do they source supercute decor at The Tot, they also sell toys and stuffed animals that are so adorable you'll actually *want* to display them.

THOMAS LAVIN SHOWROOM (thomaslavin.com)
From textiles and wall coverings to trim, lighting, and furniture, Thomas Lavin's Los Angeles showrooms feature incredible pieces sourced from around the world.

URBAN ARCHAEOLOGY (urbanarchaeology.com)
At Urban Archaeology, you can find crazy-cool salvage pieces from past centuries, or you can custom design lighting to perfectly fit your own vision.

URBAN ELECTRIC (urbanelectricco.com)
Urban Electric is one of my favorite sources for light fixtures, all of which are manufactured in the United States.

WATERWORKS (waterworks.com)
The bathroom and kitchen materials, hardware, and lighting selections at Waterworks are so beautifully curated that you can find something as simple or as ornate as you could possibly want.

With Carly Kuhn (center) and Brigette Romanek (right)

ACKNOWLEDGMENTS

I'd like to extend sincere gratitude to all those involved in creating this
book. A special thanks goes to my clients, my colleagues, and everyone who has contributed
to making the houses I've worked on truly inspiring homes. I couldn't do my job
without the designers, wholesalers, and store owners who help me source the beautiful
objects that complete every project. My goal for this book was to put a spotlight
on all that we've achieved together.

Sasha Alexander

Jessica Biel

Justin Coit

Yolanda Cuomo

Aliza Fogelson

Douglas Friedman

Heather Leeds Greenfield

Sibylle Kazeroid

Carly Kuhn

Ludo Lefebvre

Lea Michele

Charles Miers

Ashley Olsen

Mary-Kate Olsen

Ellen Pompeo

Bobbie Richardson

Whitney Robinson

Lynn Scrabis

Christina Shanahan

PHOTOGRAPHY

Patrick Cline: 55, 64, 65, 85, 97, 141, 143, 175

Justin Coit: 16-17, 18, 19, 21, 22-23, 25, 29, 32-33, 37, 42-43, 48-49, 51, 54, 56-57, 68-69,
72, 88-89, 93, 95, 96, 100-101, 110-111, 124-125, 127, 136, 137, 144, 145, 149, 156-157, 159, 166-167, 176-177,
194-195, 197, 204-205, 210-211, 230-231, 238-239

Roger Davies: 6, 76-77, 122-123, 170-171, 172-173

Douglas Friedman: 14-15, 26-27, 30-31, 34-35, 36, 39, 40, 41, 50, 52-53, 58, 60-61, 66-67,
71, 73, 79, 91, 108, 109, 115, 116-117, 118-119, 120-121, 132, 133, 139, 153, 155, 160-161, 163, 179, 182-183,
202-203, 207, 214-215, 228-229, 234-235, 242-243

Gentl and Hyers: 45, 87, 98, 209

Ian Hanson: 186, 187, 188-189, 191

Nick Johnson: 74-75, 129, 236-237, 241

Stefanie Keenan/Getty Images for Rachel Zoe Collection: 92

Michael Muller: 88 (left)

John Phillips/Getty Images for GUCCI: 90

Lisa Romerein/OTTO: 2, 102-103, 152, 169, 185, 192-193, 201, 213

Christopher Patey: 112, 113, 135, 174, 217, 218-219, 220, 223 (top and bottom), 233

Bryony Shearmur: 62-63, 146-147, 164-165, 240, 245

Brick Stowell: 224-225

STYLING AND DESIGN

Photography shoots styled by Brigette Romanek: 18-23, 25, 29-31, 33-35, 39-41, 45-49, 54-62, 73-75,
79, 81, 99, 101-102, 107, 121-123, 127, 147, 150, 159, 161-167, 172, 181, 209, 211, 216-217, 224-225, 236-239, 242, 246

Homes designed in collaboration with Brigette Romanek for Hancock Designs: 20-23, 29-31,
38-39, 48-49, 54-55, 102, 145, 150, 172-173, 208-209, 232-233, 238-239, 246-247

First published in the United States of America in 2019 by
Rizzoli International Publications, Inc.
300 Park Avenue South
New York, NY 10010
www.rizzoliusa.com

Publisher: Charles Miers
Editor: Aliza Fogelson
Book Designer: Yolanda Cuomo Design
Associate Designer: Bonnie Briant
Junior Designer: Bobbie Richardson
Design Assistant: Morgan Sloan
Production Manager: Barbara Sadick
Managing Editor: Lynn Scrabis

Printed in China

2019 2020 2021 2022 / 10 9 8 7 6 5 4 3 2 1

ISBN-13: 978-0-8478-6533-8
Library of Congress Catalog Control Number: 2019937291

Visit us online:
Facebook.com/RizzoliNewYork
Twitter: @Rizzoli_Books
Instagram.com/RizzoliBooks
Pinterest.com/RizzoliBooks
Youtube.com/user/RizzoliNY
Issuu.com/Rizzoli

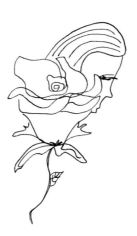